you ask about...

RELATiONSHiPS

Questions Teens are asking

by Tim **Pauls**

CONCORDIA PUBLISHING HOUSE · SAINT LOUIS

D0391658

Copyright © 2007
Concordia Publishing House,
3558 S. Jefferson Avenue,
St. Louis, MO 63118-3968
www.cph.org 1-800-325-3040

Unless otherwise indicated Scripture quotations are from The Holy Bible,
English Standard Version®. Copyright © 2001 by Crossway Bibles, a pub-
lishing ministry of Good News Publishers, Wheaton, Illinois. Used by per-
mission. All rights reserved.
Scripture quotations marked NKJV are taken from the New King James
Version®. Copyright © 1982 by Thomas Nelson, Inc. Used by permission.
All rights reserved.

Luther's Small Catechism with Explanation, © 1986, 1991, 2005
Concordia Publishing House.

Library of Congress Cataloging-in-Publication Data
Pauls, Tim, 1967-
You ask about relationships: questions teens are asking / by Tim Pauls.
   p. cm.
ISBN 978-0-7586-1007-2
ISBN 0-7586-1007-6

1. Lutheran youth--Religious life--Miscellanea. 2. Theology,
Doctrinal--Miscellanea. 3. Lutheran Church--Missouri
Synod--Doctrines--Miscellanea. I. Title.
BX8074.Y68P38 2006
230'.41--dc23

                                          2005038048

1 2 3 4 5 6 7 8 9 10   15 14 13 12 11 10 09 08 07 06

For Noah, who seems to start every relationship on the right foot. A second son like you makes me doubly blessed.

My thanks again to Pastor Mike McCoy for his suggestions, corrections, edits, and partnership in the ministry of the Gospel.

Table of Contents

So!
You Came Back

This is *You Ask*—Volume 2. Volume 1, *You Ask about Life,* covered all sorts of questions about life, including government, creation, cloning, and more. But there was one thing we didn't talk about much at all—relationships. That's because the good editors at Concordia thought that relationships could take up a whole book by itself. Boy, howdy, they were right! Here it is—a start, anyway.

you ask about . . . RELATIONSHIPS

Whether you realize it or not, you're in enough different relationships to strangle a full-grown yak. A relationship, after all, is simply a connection between two people, so you've got a bunch of them to worry about: you have a relationship with God, with family, with friends, with enemies, with people of the same sex, and people of the opposite sex. Unless you're living alone on a deserted island, you've got a lot of relationships to think about. You're probably going to have some questions. There are a bunch of them out there.

As I mentioned in the first volume, there are far more answers out there than actual questions. This sounds like a good deal at first, until you realize that most of the answers are actually wrong. A bad answer doesn't help. In fact, it often hurts. You want answers that are true.

This leads me to the big flashing DANGER sign when it comes to discussing relationships: *relationship* comes from the same root word as *relative*. I'm not talking about relatives like Uncle Beauregard or Cousin Quigley. I'm thinking of *relative* when it means "opposite of absolute." I'm a believer in absolute truth. God says some things are right while some are wrong; some are holy while others are sinful. Many people believe truth is relative—that truth changes based upon the situation. For instance:

> **Absolute truth:** "It's wrong to steal."

> **Relative truth:** "It's wrong to steal, unless it's from a big company that would waste it anyway."

Or, as we said in *You Ask about Life:*

> **Absolute truth:** "Abortion is wrong."

> **Relative truth:** "Abortion is right or wrong, depending on the opinion of the mother."

Here's one we get to talk about in this book:

> **Absolute truth:** "Premarital sex is sinful."

> **Relative truth:** "Premarital sex is okay, as long as you think you're ready for it."

See the difference? Absolute truth talks about right and wrong. Relative truth says something may be right or wrong depending on the circumstances. If that's true, then there really isn't any such thing as right and wrong.

10

When it comes to relationships, a lot of people believe everything is relative. You should do what you believe is right for you at that time, in that situation. Forget the "Thou shalts" and "Thou shalt nots" God says, and decide for yourself. It gets scary pretty quick. This book isn't going to do that.

Instead we're going to speak about relationships using some tools that God provides: these witnesses either proclaim absolute truth or submit to it. These are the same witnesses that we used in the first book, namely:

Scripture   **Common sense**

Science   **Conscience**

We talked about these in *You Ask about Life* at length, so here's a quick refresher course on the purposes and limitations of each of these witnesses.

scripture

The Bible is God's Word, written by men at His direction. The purpose of God's Word is to tell you about His plan of salvation for you. Because it is God's Word, it is without error and completely trustworthy. It is the final authority of absolute truth, of right and wrong. In His Law, God tells you a lot about all sorts of relationships, so we'll be making a lot of use of Scripture. More importantly, however, the Bible is the source of information about Jesus Christ, God's only-begotten Son who died on the cross to take away your sins.

11

The Bible has limitations—while God has given His Word to tell us about salvation, people expect the Bible to answer every question they have. Imagine this (incredibly lame) conversation:

> **Son:** Dad, I have a date and I need to borrow the car.
>
> **Dad:** Why should I loan it to you?
>
> **Son:** Because I opened my Bible to 2 Kings 9, where Jehu traveled to Jezreel. He didn't walk, but rode in a chariot. Since I'm taking Alice out on a date, I figure this is God's way of saying I shouldn't have to walk either.

Dad: As I recall, a chariot had two wheels. Maybe God is saying you should ride your bike.

Son: But it was pulled by horses, and your car has horsepower.

Dad: And yet Jehu drove that chariot furiously. I don't want you driving my car that way, so you'd better take a hike.

Son: Well, if you look . . .

Dad: No, I mean it. Take a hike. Now!

I did say that it was a lame conversation before you had to read it, but hopefully you get the point. The story of Jehu is not written by God to tell when you can borrow a car. It's a story about God's judgment on evil. Likewise, the Bible doesn't have answers to every question about life you have. (That's a reason why I'm not a fan of the popular, but fading, *WWJD* "What Would Jesus Do?" bracelets and theology. We don't know what Jesus would do a lot of the time.) Sometimes, the Bible says, "You must." Sometimes, it says, "You must not." The rest of the time, it leaves it up to you to make a good choice. If you're out on a date and have to choose between steak and chicken, don't open up your Bible to find out what the Lord wants you to order. You can do either with the Lord's blessing. (By the way, don't order rabbit if you're going out with someone who keeps them for pets. That wasn't my best dating moment.) For more on this, see "common sense" below.

12

science

Contrary to what some Christians think, or your report card says, science is not your enemy. Science is God's gift for exploring and understanding the incredible universe He has created for us. In other words, the purpose of science is to discover truth about the world around you. Without scientific study, there would be no medicine, air travel, computers, microwaves—all sorts of things we take for granted. I'm a big fan of science; and since we're part of the scientific world, science can tell us some things about ourselves.

For this book, science has two very big limitations. For one thing, since science is the study of creation, it just isn't equipped to study the Creator. Science can't tell you about God, beyond the fact He must exist. Many people today try to use science to prove God doesn't exist, or to say the Bible is wrong. As we discussed for a long time in *You Ask about Life,* this is a misuse of science and a real waste of brainpower.

13

The other limitation is relationships often involve unscientific and irrational behaviors—like having a crush on someone. Such behaviors are also outside of the realm of science. Note my comments about emotions below. We'll use a little science in this book, but not much.

common sense

God has given you an immensely practical tool in common sense, which means you have the ability to make logical conclusions about the world around you, to make decisions about things the Bible doesn't talk about. You can decide some things are true and some aren't because some things make sense while others don't. This is a great gift—you can make a far better case to borrow your parents' car with common sense than you can with Scripture. Properly used and disciplined, common sense goes a long way to help you make good decisions and keep you out of trouble. However, common sense has an important limitation—it's part of you, and you're sinful. That means you can convince yourself the sensible choice is the sinful choice, that it's sensible at times to ignore the Bible. Be careful, be sure you always submit your common sense to what Scripture says. Given God's faithfulness and truth, it only makes sense.

14

conscience

God has kindly written His law on your heart, so you have a built-in understanding of right and wrong. That's why your conscience bugs you when you do something wrong. This is a blessing, an important gift when dealing with relationships. For instance, if you don't want to tell your parents what you did on a date, it means your conscience is warning you of big trouble. However, your conscience has the same problem as common sense—it's part of you, the sinful you. It's easy enough to keep committing the same sin over and over until it doesn't bother you anymore. That doesn't mean the sin is okay, rather you've managed to grind your conscience down and dull it. It's just like common sense: if your conscience disagrees with

Scripture, you're the one who's wrong.

Those are the witnesses we'll be using to help us look at relationships. There is one witness we won't be using—emotion. Relationships are full of emotions—sometimes rather intense emotions. A lot of people believe in living by feelings. When you start to look at advice on relationships, you tend to hear a lot of silly slogans like, "you'll know when it feels right," "if it feels good, do it," "follow your feelings," or the famous song lyric, "it can't be wrong when it feels so right." Blah, blah, blah. One of the worst offenders is the idea love is a *feeling*, so you can stop loving when you stop feeling like loving. We'll get into this more later.

But for now, let me say this: I like emotions, they're part of who God made us to be. However, they're not much help when it comes to right and wrong. In other words, feelings don't tell you what's the right and wrong choice, rather how you feel about the choices. You can be attracted to the sin and angered by the right decision, but that doesn't make the sin right. Instead, it shows how prone to sin you are! Furthermore, emotions change all the time because of sleep, circumstance, energy level, and more. I'm much happier to see my kids come bounding out of their room in the morning when I've slept well than when I'm hanging by a thread and begging the coffee pot to work faster. The kids haven't changed, but my feelings have. While some maintain following emotions are the way to go, they should also remember the many murders committed in a moment of strong feelings. Don't

15

trust emotions. Use them as clues to how life is going, but don't let them make decisions for you.

I think we're about ready to move on, but here's a final thought before we go. Relationships can be messy, because they usually involve two or more sinful people. Sometimes the right decision is clear, and sometimes it's not so easy. Sometimes the Bible clearly speaks to a matter, and sometimes it doesn't. If I'm guessing at something, I'll be sure to tell you I'm giving my opinion, not binding you to something that God didn't say. Sometimes relationships will have you feeling sky-high, and sometimes they'll leave you in the dirt. But, there is one relationship that's perfectly clear. You are one for whom Christ died on the cross; therefore, no matter what else is true, you can be certain God regards you as one redeemed, and uses all things for your good.

We move on . . .

Pastor Tim Pauls

18

Section One:
Service
Station
in
Solution

To understand how relationships work, it's good to go back to the very beginning. If we look at Genesis 1–3, we find some basic principles that teach a lot about relationships: how they're supposed to work, why they don't work that way anymore, and what to do. For your memory retention pleasure, all of the following points apparently begin with the letter "S," which is just way too cutesy for me.

Service

In the beginning, there was God. God is, by His very nature, a servant. He calls Himself a helper (Hebrews 13:6). The Father serves the Son and puts all things under His feet (Ephesians 1:22). The Son serves the Father by doing His will (Matthew 26:42). The Holy Spirit is sent forth as the "Helper" (John 15:26). The almighty, all-powerful Holy Trinity desires and delights to serve. Think about that for a second. In every other religion that features some sort of divine being, the god is always demanding you serve it before it does anything to help you. But the one true God delights to serve—to give you all good things!

Because God desires to serve, He created all things and placed Adam in the Garden of Eden. God didn't create Adam because He needed help with running the universe, but to serve the man and give man everything he needed to live forever.

19

In fact, day six of the Creation was still going strong when the Lord gave Adam another gift—Eve. Look what God said, "It is not good that man should be alone; I will make him a helper comparable to him" (Genesis 2:18 NKJV). A what? A helper! A comparable helper. God created Eve to be a servant to Adam, just as Adam was created to be a servant to Eve. This is part of what it means in Genesis 1:27 when it says God created man in His own image. If you check the Explanation to the First Article of the Apostle's Creed in *Luther's Small Catechism*, you'll find this means

Adam and Eve were created to be "righteous and holy, doing God's will" (SC, p. 115). It's God's will to serve. Therefore, as His righteous and holy creation, it was the will of Adam and Eve to serve as well—to serve God as well as one another.

How would they serve? God blessed them and said to them, "Be fruitful and multiply and fill the earth and subdue it and have dominion over the fish of the sea and over the birds of the heavens and over every living thing that moves on the earth" (Genesis 1:28). He put Adam and Eve in charge of the earth. They were to have kids ("be fruitful and multiply") whom they would serve, take care of each other and subdue the earth—take care of creation.

As God created Adam and Eve to be servants, He has created you to be a servant, too. Every relationship you are in is an opportunity for service.

Station

Really? Every relationship is an opportunity for service? It seems like serving goes in only one direction—from the lowly to the powerful. Kings rule over people, commanding them to obey; it's the subjects who do all the obeying. Bosses tell employees what to do and demand results, the employees have to jump through the hoops. Teachers assign the homework and say when it's due, you're the one who's cramming for the exam. Sounds like serving is a one-way street.

That may be how it seems, and often is, in this world—but that's not how it's supposed to be.

Everyone is supposed to be serving. When God gives someone authority and makes them king or boss or teacher, He gives them their authority to serve. Kings serve their subjects by protecting them from harm. Bosses serve their employees by providing a good work environment and coordinating efforts. Teachers serve students by equipping them with knowledge for the future.

To put it another way, God gives different stations to different people in life. We need rulers, but not everyone gets to be king. Some are teachers, doctors, janitors, students. People have different stations, and some get more recognition than others—but all have opportunities to serve.

God and Adam and Eve each had different stations: God was God. Adam was man/husband/future dad, and Eve was woman/wife/future mom. Each knew God's will for their stations. Adam and Eve, each knew their limitations—a man's a man and a woman's a woman, the two aren't the same. God entrusted His Word to Adam to preach to Eve and whatever kids came along (Genesis 2:16–17), while He gave Eve the extraordinary gift and privilege of bearing children and bringing life into the world. Because there was no sin in the world, this was not a problem. Before the fall, Adam wouldn't have said, "Since God is a servant, I'll make Him do things according to my will, not His." To say that would reject the station of (created) "man" that God had given him. Without sin, Adam wouldn't do this. Instead, he'd quite happily confess God had the station of God, which meant God's will

21

was always right. Likewise, Adam wouldn't say, "I'm tired of being the man, so I want to be the one who has the kids." Nor would Eve say, "I don't like the station of future mom, so I want to take over Adam's station instead." Holy and righteous, each was thankful God made them who they were in order to fulfill the stations God gave them. Without sin, those stations were easy to do.

Such was life in the garden before the fall. Imagine what it would have been like. Adam would be constantly working to make sure that Eve was doing well, and Eve would be constantly working to take care of Adam. When the kids came along, they'd be busy serving their parents and looking out for each other, while the parents were happily taking care of them. No fights. No arguments. No hurt feelings.

22

So God created Adam and Eve to serve, just like Him. God gave them stations in which they would serve Him and each other. That's how God set up relationships to work. He created you to serve, and He has given you stations in life from which to serve. Your stations right now may include son or daughter; brother or sister; boyfriend or girlfriend; student, employee, friend, and so forth. In each of these stations God gives you the opportunity to serve—even as He serves you.

It's really very simple. Keep service and station in their proper perspective, and relationships are a snap.

Except for one problem! Sin has come into the world.

Sin

"Now the serpent was more crafty than any other beast of the field that the Lord God had made. He said to the woman, 'Did God actually say, "You shall not eat of any tree in the garden"?' " (Genesis 3:1). When Eve repeated God's warning, the devil went on, "You will not surely die. For God knows that when you eat of it your eyes will be opened, and you will be like God, knowing good and evil" (Genesis 3:4–5). You know what happened: Eve listened and ate the deadly fruit. Then she handed some to Adam, standing right next to her, and he ate, too.

The consequences were severe. You've read them before, but read them again with "service" and "station" in mind, because this is really important for the rest of the book—sin really, really messed up serving and station, and so sin really messed up relationships.

To Eve, God said, "I will surely multiply your pain in childbearing; in pain you shall bring forth children" (Genesis 3:16). From now on, because of sin, every God-given station was going to be tough. There are few joys more awesome and powerful than watching a baby being born—this is how God brings life into the world. But having witnessed this miracle twice with the birth of my kids, my wife went through an awful lot of pain in her station of "mom" those days. It was a somber reminder that we live in a world of pain and death, another reason to get children to the font and baptized ASAP.

23

The Lord also told Eve, "Your desire shall be for your husband, and he shall rule over you" (Genesis 3:16). Briefly, He meant this: from now on, Adam and Eve wouldn't want to serve each other. Eve would desire her husband submit to her sinful will and demands, and Adam would return the favor and desire to rule over Eve, demanding that she serve him.

This is a biggie when it comes to relationships: before the fall into sin, people (all two of them) were naturally servants. Once sin arrived, all people would be naturally selfish. Instead of desiring to serve, they would desire to be served. And let me tell you, in any relationship, selfishness is a leading killer.

24

To Adam, God said,

> Because you have listened to the voice of your wife and have eaten of the tree of which I commanded you, "You shall not eat of it," cursed is the ground because of you; in pain you shall eat of it all the days of your life; thorns and thistles it shall bring forth for you; and you shall eat the plants of the field. By the sweat of your face you shall eat bread, till you return to the ground, for out of it you were taken; for you are dust, and to dust you shall return. **(Genesis 3:17–19)**

Adam listened to Eve and ate the fruit, instead of

listening to the Lord: he rejected stations and decided Eve knew better than God. As a result, all of his daily labors would be cursed with pain and sweat, thorns and thistles—it's uncanny how much that sounds like mowing my lawn! Instead of enjoying eternal life, he'd have to work hard just to survive for a while.

The final consequence was death, Adam and all people would return to the dust. "For the wages of sin is death," begins Romans 6:23. It's true, everything dies. Plants wither and stars supernova. Animals die and people do, too. Thanks to sin, relationships are destined to die as well, one way or another.

Sin works to separate, to isolate, and to destroy relationships. As soon as Adam and Eve sinned, they were separated from God. The Lord came to walk with them in the cool of the day, and instead had to expel them from the garden. Furthermore, that sinful selfishness would drive a wedge between the two. The more selfish Adam and Eve became, the more they would only look out for themselves and the less they would trust each other. Selfishness and distrust hurt relationships badly.

Sin isolates. God created Eve because it was not good for Adam to be alone. Sin agrees, and so it seeks to make Adam and Eve lonely again. Here are a few examples:

> ✽ Two girls have been good friends since 3rd grade. In 8th grade, they both get a crush on the same guy. Because they each want to get his attention, they start competing against

25

each other growing jealous of each other. Neither one gets the guy, but by the end of it they aren't talking to each other. They're isolated.

✱ Tempted to be selfish, a man spends all of his weekends away from his family, hanging out with the guys and playing with his ATV or his fishing gear. He and his wife grow apart, and she finally files for divorce because they're two strangers living under one roof. Now they live in two separate homes, and the kids are always separated from one parent or the other, isolated.

✱ A man loses his wife to cancer after thirty-five years of marriage, so they're separated by death and the grave. He lives in a big, lonely house surrounded by memories and grief. His friends, afraid of saying something stupid, decide it's best to leave him alone. He's trapped in a terrible isolation of grief and loneliness.

✱ A grandmother falls and breaks her hip. She used to go out for a walk and chat with the neighbors or drive to a quilting club at church, now she can't get out anymore. She's stuck at home with few visitors. Sin has worked sickness and injury, so she's all alone.

✱ A young woman breaks off her engagement after finding her fiancé has been cheating on her. Even though she's done the right thing by separating, she's going to have a hard time trusting anyone for a long time. She might decide it's better to be lonely than to risk the pain again.

✱ A Christian man falls in love with a woman who isn't a believer. Bedazzled by her charm, he moves in with her instead of getting married. They live happily for years . . . except his guilt about their immorality keeps him from going to church, and he drifts away from the faith. He's united with a beautiful woman . . . but he's separated from God.

27

The loneliness only grows as the wages of sin—death—kicks in. People grieve when a loved one dies, as they become isolated from a mother or a brother or a child.

The greatest separation sin brings is hell—eternal separation from God and His gifts of grace, life and salvation. In Matthew 22:1–14, Jesus compares His kingdom to a wedding banquet. The King invites all who will come into the banquet hall for the feast and the celebration. Those who, for whatever reason, do not want to be with the king remain outside—in "the outer darkness. In that place there will be weeping and gnashing of teeth" (Matthew 22:13). Where my finite mind has trouble imagining heaven and hell, such parables teach me. Inside heaven is the banquet feast, where the people of God are together for eternity, free from all the sin that divides and kills and isolates. Those who reject the Lord are trapped in hell, where sin and distrust and isolation remain forever.

If you want proof of sin in this world, examine the relationships around you. The best of marriages has sore points and rough spots. Brothers and sisters fight from the earliest of ages. Friendships disintegrate— sometimes spectacularly. Everybody feels lonely and isolated from time to time, and the panic only grows when they realize the sin that brings this loneliness is also bringing death. That's quite the enemy to fight and overcome. In fact, you and I can't do it. But there is a solution.

Solution

The solution for this sinful isolation is Jesus Christ, the Son of the living God. Rather than leave us lost and isolated in sin, God sent His only Son into the world to be the Savior. Rather than leave us lonely and dying far away, Jesus became flesh to dwell among us (John 1:14) and save us. Look at what He did for your salvation. He placed every sin that separates you from God upon Himself and took it to the cross. Since death separates you from the living, He died in your place. He went to the grave to break its bands, to deliver you from its isolation. He even descended into hell to proclaim His victory, to declare that you would not be imprisoned there for an eternity of outer darkness, but raised up to the wedding feast of heaven. Instead of leaving you lost and lonely, Christ came and sacrificed Himself to redeem you and make you God's child once more. For Jesus' sake, God says to you who were not His people, "You are Mine—forever!" (See Hosea 1:10.)

The saving work of Jesus defeats sin and the isolation it brings, the Bible uses all sorts of "together" words to describe it. Look at Holy Baptism, where God makes you His own child. There, by water and Word, God transforms you from sinful orphan to beloved child—part of His family. He brings you into Church—the communion of saints—where you now have a hundredfold of mothers and brothers and sisters (Mark 10:30). He brings you to the altar for Holy Communion, where—far from separated from God because of sin—the Son of God gives you His body and blood for the forgiveness of sins. Where there is forgiveness of sins, there is also life and salvation.

29

Do you see? What sin separated, stole and destroyed, Jesus restored by His life, death and resurrection!

Of course, at this point you still live in a sinful world where relationships are still tarnished and troubled. By the grace of God, you walk by faith and not by sight—a good thing, since your sight sees a lot of sin and messed-up relationships. But by faith, you know your Savior has won the victory for you and rescued you from the death and isolation that sin brings.

As He forgives you, He also gives you the grace to

live as a servant in the stations and relationships that you have. As St. John says, "We love because He first loved us" (1 John 4:19).

Until the Lord returns, you and I are stuck in a world of sin where relationships are tough, but the Lord gives us help in His Word. His Law is full of all sorts of commandments that are helpful. Just look at the Ten Commandments, where a quick index might go like this:

You and God: The First, Second and Third Commandments.

You and your parents, teachers, bosses and other authorities: The Fourth Commandment.

30

You and friends, colleagues, enemies and annoying magazine salesmen: The Fifth through Tenth Commandments.

These Commandments govern relationships, establish stations and call for servanthood. Take, for instance, the Fourth Commandment, "You shall honor your father and your mother." This reminds you of your station as "son" or "daughter." You serve them when you "honor them, serve and obey them, love and cherish them" (SC, p. 74).

We'll be referring to these and other laws from the Bible as we look at different relationships, but be warned: the primary purpose of God's Law is not to make you avoid pitfalls and be good at relationships. The purpose of God's Law is to show you your sin and your need for a Savior . . . and your relationships with others will often demonstrate how sinful and selfish you are.

That's why the Law and relationship advice aren't the end of the story: if they are, then we're condemned. No, Jesus is the end of the story, because He forgives you and promises—no matter how rocky are your relationships here—your life with Him is guaranteed forever.

Service—Station—Sin—Solution. If you want it all summed up in Scripture:

> But Jesus called them to Him and said, "You know that the rulers of the Gentiles lord it over them, and their great ones exercise authority over them. It shall not be so among you. But whoever would be great among you must be your servant, and whoever would be first among you must be your slave, even as the Son of Man came not to be served but to serve, and to give His life as a ransom for many." **(Matthew 20:25–28).**

31

To match it with the four "S's"

STATION:

"You know that the rulers of the Gentiles . . ."

SIN:

". . . lord it over them . . ."

SERVICE:
"But whoever would be great among you must be your servant, and whoever would be first among you must be your slave . . ."

SOLUTION:
". . . even as the Son of Man came not to be served but to serve, and to give His life as a ransom for many."

As you seek to serve others in your station, confess your sin and rejoice in this, the Son of Man came not to be served by you, but to serve you. By His death, you are ransomed for eternal life. That's the relationship He establishes with you, and He will not fail.

32

34 Section Two:
YOU

Nope! We're not ready to talk about relationships yet. Before you can deal with others, you've got to be able to live with yourself. This may or may not seem like an easy thing to do. After all, if you're reading this book it means that you're probably around junior high or high school age, which I personally found to be exciting, annoying, and nerve-wracking. Except for the first year of your life, when you were a blob and all you cared about was eating and drooling, your body is undergoing more violent physical changes than it ever will naturally again. You're not the little kid who used to stick pencils up his nose in third grade. You might be the big kid who sticks pencils up his nose, but that's a whole different story.

You're becoming more independent. For years now, your parents have been gradually training you to become independent so you can eventually be a self-sufficient adult. Right now, you have some freedoms and some restrictions—and this may be a major source of friction between you and your parents.

Raging hormones might have you looking at life and people differently, and quite likely doing some stupid things from time to time. Others might find you annoying. You might even be annoying yourself, and every mistake you make makes you feel like there's a spotlight on you.

Is it really possible to like yourself and hate yourself at the same time? Welcome to the joy of the transitional teenage years.

To get to know you, let's first set down some basic, objective truths and then answer some questions about identity.

1. You have objective worth: you're irreplaceable and priceless. Hear what David says as he speaks God's Word:

> For You formed my inward parts; You

knitted me together in my mother's
womb. I praise You, for I am fearfully
and wonderfully made. Wonderful are
Your works; my soul knows it very
well. My frame was not hidden from
You, when I was being made in secret,
intricately woven in the depths of the
earth. **(Psalm 139:13–15)**

God put you together exactly as He desired you to
be, for use as His instrument. You are priceless:

You were ransomed from the futile
ways inherited from your forefathers,
not with perishable things such as
silver or gold, but with the precious
blood of Christ, like that of a lamb
without blemish or spot.
(1 Peter 1:18–19)

36

God redeemed you from sin at the price of His
Son's blood and death on the cross. This means, no
matter what you or anybody else thinks—no matter
how worthless you feel or have been made to feel—
you have an objective worth. God values you so much
that He's given His Son to die for you. That's seriously different from how the rest of the world thinks.

A lot of people are obsessed with theories of evolution, which is far more of a religion than any sort of
scientific logic. (For more information see *You Asked
about Life* where we spent a lot of time discussing the
theory of evolution.) Anyway, evolution teaches
everything is pretty much an accident: the earth just
happened to land the right distance from the sun with

all the right ingredients for life, which just happened to somehow get started and lead to all sorts of life-forms today. According to evolution, everything is just an accident. This includes you. You're just the way a bunch of DNA happened to mix together to come up with you. Naturally, not all accidents are equal. Some people will naturally be stronger, smarter and better-looking than others—if that's you, lucky you! But you're still an accident waiting to die. If it's not, then it's just too bad, you're not worth as much as the beautiful people. So goes your worth according to evolution.

Atheism does the same thing. If there's no God doing the creating, then you're just an accident with no intrinsic worth. When God doesn't establish your value, then it's up to other people to decide how much you're worth. If you have strength or smarts or beauty, then you're worth something. If you don't—or if you're old or disabled, then you're not worth as much. In fact, you may be a liability who should simply be killed in order to "help society." If you look at the twentieth century, you'll find the greatest mass murderers included Joseph Stalin, Adolph Hitler, Mao Zedong and Pol Pot. What did these tyrants have in common? They all denied the existence of God. Therefore, they got to decide who was worth letting live and who wasn't.

In many other religions, you don't have objective worth, you're only worth as much as you earn. In Islam, Allah loves you if you keep enough rules. In Hinduism, obedience leads to a better reincarnation—

37

maybe you can come back as a cow! In other religions, the god says, "I'll look at how you act and decide how much you're worth."

The fact that we all have a value marks Christianity as completely different from any other religion, according to the Bible, God looks at you and says, "No matter what you do, I've already decided you're worth so much that I've already given My Son to die on the cross for you."

So when we start talking about you, we start with this truth: you're not a worthless accident. You're unique, irreplaceable, and of priceless worth.

Of course, sin always has to come along and mess things up, which leads us to our next truth.

38

2. You're sinful!

Even though you are redeemed by Jesus and set free from sin to do good works, that old sinful nature of yours is still hanging around, tempting you to all sorts of sins. Furthermore, sin affects every part of you. You may have been born with a birth defect, suffered an early injury that affects you for life, or be afflicted with scarring acne, and the like. There will be limitations on your strength, health, looks, and intelligence, all brought about by sin.

Old Adam is doing his evil best to use these things to make you doubt your worth, making you a confused mess in the meantime. There will be things you don't like about yourself because you will do the wrong things—never underestimate your ability to do or say something stupid. There will be things about you that you really like—even though they are sinful. There will be parts of you that you don't like because you're busy coveting who somebody else is and resenting who God made you to be. Instead of giving thanks for the talents and abilities God *has* given you, it will always be much easier to complain about the ones He *hasn't*.

If you listen to Old Adam long enough, you'll end up basing your worth on who you are and who you aren't, the talents you have and the ones that you don't. Go down that road, and you'll likely suffer from either self-hatred or extreme pride, both of which lead to Old Adam's ultimate goal: death and separation from God forever. That's why it's so important daily to confess your sins and remember that Christ died and rose again to redeem you.

3. Life isn't fair.

It's not! The more you expect it to be, the more you're going to be disappointed. It's not fair that a child is born with fetal alcohol syndrome because the mother drank too much. It's not fair that celebrities make millions for immorality while churches suffer financial woes. It's not fair that a tornado hits one town and spares another. It's not fair that some children grow up in good families, while others suffer abuse. The world *isn't* fair . . . it *is* sinful.

Therefore, the world isn't going to be fair to you. There will be times when you do everything right and your efforts come crashing down. There will be times when somebody does everything wrong and still profits from it. You're not going to be good at everything, many of your talents may be hidden. Not everybody is going to like you. In fact, if you're going to stand for anything, get used to the idea that many people aren't going to like you. You may be born with a disability. You may grow up in a poverty-stricken area that doesn't help you prepare for the future. It's not fair, but that's how it is.

Come to think of it, God isn't fair, either. "Fair" would mean *you* pay for your sin. It's nowhere near fair for Jesus to suffer on the cross for the sins of the world. It's not fair at all for God to say you're priceless because of your righteousness, when you're only righteous because Jesus sacrificed Himself for you. It's not fair that salvation is free.

The longer I'm alive, the more I give thanks God isn't fair!

4. When it comes to your own identity, there are two huge dangers to your faith.

Proverbs 30:8–9 clues us in:

> Remove far from me falsehood and lying; give me neither poverty nor riches; feed me with the food that is

> needful for me, lest I be full and deny
> You and say, "Who is the Lord?" or
> lest I be poor and steal and profane
> the name of my God.

It's an honest observation about the temptations of wealth. If someone has too much money, they tend to get proud and see no need for God. If someone has too little, they tend to believe God isn't looking out for them. The same temptations apply to whom God made you to be, so be on the lookout.

One temptation is to love yourself too much. You may be blessed with gifts that make you popular with others—looks, money, humor, charm, muscle, whatever. It's nice to be popular and well-liked by others. In fact, it feels a whole lot better than being unpopular and not liked. However, your old sinful nature—often popular, always ugly—will use this. Old Adam does his best to make you proud of the things that make you popular. As your pride grows you start to take personal credit for everything. You live, act, and think as if you alone are responsible for these gifts, as if God had nothing to do with them.

On your way down this path, you'll eventually lose a lot of friends. But sin is after something even greater, it wants you to trust so completely in yourself that you dump the Lord completely. Then you can be pretty, rich, funny, charming, strong . . . and going to hell. Hey, the devil doesn't mind if you enjoy the ride, as long as you get there.

The other danger is to hate who you are. You may not have a set of gifts that makes you popular. You may have been born with disabilities or conditions that keep you from reaching the goals and hopes you have for yourself. Old Adam can put this to good use, too. He'll go ahead and tempt you to ignore Jesus' death on the cross (for you!) and lead you to believe God must not love you as much as others, maybe not at all. If God doesn't love you, what do you need God for? Maybe you ought to pack your bags and leave the Savior behind. When you leave the Savior behind, you're headed for eternal judgment once again.

Any pastor will tell you a lot of youth are leaving the church these days. After confirmation instruction, they fade away. Given the messages society bombards you with, the temptation is understandable. Those who are blessed with popularity and intelligence fade away because the world is their oyster, and they see no need to spend time confessing their sin when they feel so good about themselves. Those who are not so blessed may find fault with God for creating them the way they are, and don't see how the Lord's gift of grace is going to help them now. For all sorts of reasons, they leave. Some come back. Some don't; if they don't repent, they're lost forever.

Whoever the Lord has made you to be, you can be certain of His love and faithfulness to you because He's already given His Son to die in your place on the cross. Whatever the skills and shortcomings you have, you are His instrument for His purposes. Always remember that your identity begins at the cross, where Jesus died to make you His beloved child forever.

5. The greatest treasures receive the least praise in this world.

How much respect does Jesus receive in the world today for His death on the cross? Not much. In fact, most of the world goes around denying the fact that His sacrifice for the sins of the world is important at all. How much praise does the Lord receive for Holy Baptism or Holy Communion? Even within Church, these gifts are downplayed by many people, even though they are God's means by which He gives us forgiveness and faith, eternal life, and salvation! Are people thankful for the Lord's gift of His Word, so we might know of His love and salvation for us? Nope. The world sees the Bible as restrictive and intolerant. That's the way of the world. The really important treasures receive little praise and are often scorned, while trivial things and sinfulness get glorified.

It is the same way with your world. The fallen world likes flash, glamour, and sin. The gangsta rapper with the foul mouth is going to get a lot more attention in the news than the college student who writes great papers. The starlet who takes her clothes off is going to sell more posters and get a lot more media coverage than the girl who is saving her virginity for marriage.

But what is good in the eyes of God? Now, you may not be looking to record a CD with your posse, but I find that a lot of youth are critical of themselves because they don't have talents that make them stand

43

out: they're not the fastest, strongest, smartest, pretti-
est, funniest, and on and on. While these gifts are nice,
there are better ones. Consider Proverbs 31:30,
"Charm is deceitful, and beauty is vain, but a woman
who fears the Lord is to be praised." What's really
important? Things that last eternally! In the meantime,
character traits like faithfulness, gentleness, and
humility may not be flashy, but they're far better than
infidelity, coarse behavior, and pride.

6. Remember chapter 1?

God created you to be a servant. That's your identity, a beloved child of God, forgiven for Jesus' sake to
serve others.

44

Keeping all of this in mind, let's answer a few questions about you.

How do i know God loves me personally?

Because He says so! One of my favorite parts of the Christmas story is when the angel appears to the shepherds in the field and says, "For unto you is born this day in the city of David a Savior, who is Christ the Lord" (Luke 2:11). Not, "For all the world," which is true, but "unto you." The Lord sends an angel to tell lowly shepherds the Savior is born for them! Likewise, He says, "I baptize you in the name of the Father and of the Son and of the Holy Spirit." In Holy Baptism, the Lord of all specifically targets you with His favor and grace. Likewise, in Absolution, He doesn't say through the pastor, "I forgive all the repentant people." He says, "I forgive you."

i just don't like myself very much. What do i do?

That's a pretty open-ended question, but I'm willing to bet that most teenagers feel this way a lot of the time. Like it or not, you're in a decade-long struggle to figure out who you are. For one thing, it's tough to know who you are when you're changing physically—when you can't even trust your body to be the same tomorrow. You're probably worried about what others think about you since you see yourself as a mess. So along with what we said before, remember you are often your own worst critic. You see all your mistakes, while everybody else only sees a few. You get to deal with all the confusion in your mind; they don't.

That's pretty much how I felt when I was starting high school. It wasn't especially fun. Normal, sure, but not fun. So what do you do? Remember you are the Lord's own child. No matter how *you* feel about *you*, *He* loves you enough to have died for you already. Remember you're in a turbulent few years that will even out. When you do something klutzy or wrong, use it as an antidote against pride. You will have a much easier life if you understand your sins and limitations rather than cruising through high school believing you're invincible.

Remember, invincible high schoolers often get "un-invincibililized" in the real world later. Meanwhile you've gotten over it. Imagine the jock who cut classes in high school and suddenly finds he's not all that talented in college athletics, while others are pulling high grades and preparing for a well-paying job.

In the meantime, stay faithful to the Word and keep going to Church, where your Savior works through His Word and Sacraments to strengthen your faith. The Son of God conquered death for you. Born to Mary and fully human, He endured puberty—without sin—and survived. You're going to be okay.

47

Why did God give me a disability?

In this world, life is going to be a struggle for everyone since sin tries to ruin everything. In some cases, this means a disability—like a birth defect or a later injury. Disabilities can afflict your body or your mind. It's safe to say disabilities are going to make success in this world tougher. Like you need me to tell you this!

I can't tell you why the Lord allowed you to be disabled—no one can—the Lord doesn't reveal such secrets in this life. If you spend your life trying to find what God doesn't say, there's a big possibility you're going to miss what He does tell you. Take, for instance, St. Paul in 2 Corinthians:

> So to keep me from being too elated
> by the surpassing greatness of the rev-
> elations, a thorn was given me in the
> flesh, a messenger of Satan to harass
> me, to keep me from being too elat-
> ed. Three times I pleaded with the
> Lord about this, that it should leave
> me. But He said to me, "My grace is
> sufficient for you, for My power is
> made perfect in weakness." Therefore
> I will boast all the more gladly of my
> weaknesses, so that the power of
> Christ may rest upon me.
> **(2 Corinthians 12:7–9)**

48 St. Paul had a thorn. We don't know what it was, but it was something that held him back, got in his way, and frustrated him. He pleaded with the Lord to get rid of it, but God didn't for a reason; as long as Paul had this thorn, it constantly reminded him he should trust Jesus, not himself. If Paul trusted Paul, Paul was a goner. If Paul trusted Jesus, he had eternal life. That's why he went on to say, "For the sake of Christ, then, I am content with weaknesses, insults, hardships, persecutions, and calamities. For when I am weak, then I am strong" (2 Corinthians 12:10). If our weaknesses lead us to trust in Jesus, this is a great strength indeed.

Here's the peculiar blessing that comes with dis-abilities and other shortcomings. They teach you, in a way far more effective than a sermon, that you can't rely on yourself. They teach you that you need a

Savior, and your Savior has promised to restore you fully for eternity. Be warned: the devil will use things like disabilities to convince you God especially hates you, but it's not so. You have God's Word of His love for you, He's redeemed you with His own Son's blood, and He will raise you from the dead, fully healed, on the Last Day.

if God loves me, how come i stink at math?

Read the question above about disabilities. It may be you're just not doing the work, but it may be you're just not gifted with numbers. While bombing geometry isn't nearly as serious as a permanent disability, it still demonstrates the fact you have limitations. You have weaknesses. You have shortcomings. In a sinful world, you're not going to be good at everything. Here's something important to think about, something that will affect your outlook for years to come. When you run into a brick wall because of your shortcomings, you can grow bitter about it, believing God let you down. Or, you can use it to remind you that you need Jesus as your Savior, and then go and figure out what talents the Lord *has* given you. I recommend the second.

i'm thinking of getting a tattoo. What does the Bible say?

Tattoos are big these days, especially with all those

49

people clamoring to have "I Love Martin Luther" inscribed on their bodies.

The Bible mentions tattoos in Leviticus 19:28, where they are strictly forbidden. However, while God gave this command to His people in the Old Testament, He doesn't renew it in the New. Therefore, though this may alarm your mom, I can't say that the Bible forbids you from getting a tattoo. Keep in mind, though, as far as religion goes, tattoos are associated with pagan religions—not Christianity. As I recall, pagan worshipers would sometimes have a tattoo of their favorite god's name, signifying whom they were dedicated to serve. Even today, you have to prize something pretty highly before you pay to have it permanently inscribed on your skin. On the other hand, Christians received the invisible mark of Holy Baptism, signifying who had chosen them.

Here's one law that certainly does apply:

> Children, obey your parents in the Lord, for this is right. "Honor your father and mother" (this is the first commandment with a promise), that it may go well with you and that you may live long in the land.
> (Ephesians 6:1–3)

Even though the Bible is quiet on this issue, your parents probably have some good reasons why you shouldn't go for the tattoo. Consider some reasons from science and common sense.

Your skin is designed by God to keep lots of bad things out and keep you healthy. Tattooing involves injecting dyes, some containing metals, into your skin. Experts aren't sure this is a real good thing to be doing. Furthermore, the tattooing process can also bring about bacterial infection, hepatitis, and other nasty diseases. Excessive tattooing is considered a form of self-mutilation, indicating a desire to punish oneself and the need for some serious counseling (see the question on cutting below).

We should look at the science of economics, also. Tattoos are expensive, with reputable artists charging well over $100 an hour. That's cheap—compared to the cost of having a tattoo removed, which brings us to the common sense argument against tattooing.

Common sense says this: get some old family albums out and look at the pictures of you. You're likely going to find your parents dressed you in some outfits you wouldn't be caught in dead today. Now, imagine that you're still wearing one of those outfits, complete with the picture of the dancing pink bunny rabbits and the words, "I want my mommy now!" Mortifying! Now imagine you have to pay a few thousand dollars and suffer immense pain before you can change into another outfit.

I'm betting you've gotten some clothes in the last two years that you've vowed you'll never wear again. Tattoos are pretty much a permanent deal, and what looks cool today is going to look faded and stretched in a few years' time. Do you really, really want to do this to yourself?

51

What about body-piercing?

If you're going for body-piercing, I recommend a variety of ring sizes so that you can play them like a xylophone.

Seriously, ear-piercing has been around at least since Jacob and Esau (Genesis 35:4), and earrings can enhance beauty. But somewhere between two and ten, the number of piercings in an ear gets to be too much. How come? Some people will say it's just a matter of personal taste, but let me ask you this: Why would you want to get pierced?

Piercings often send a message. As I said before, one or two in the ears often enhances beauty, while some piercings are intended purely for shock value. Like a bunch of steel hoops in your ear with a chain running to your nose. Others convey sexual messages. While others, like excessive tattooing, are considered to be a form of self-mutilation. Indeed, I've run into a few testimonials from people who get pierced to experience the pain of running a needle through body parts. This isn't beauty enhancement, but an indication that self-destruction could be in the works.

In my opinion, the "why" of a piercing is more important than the "where" or the "how many." If you know who you are and you're comfortable with that, those questions won't even need to be asked.

Tongue-cleaving?

Yuck. Tongue cleaving is a step beyond excessive piercing: it's the splitting of one's tongue partway down the middle to make it forked like a snake. Highly disturbing, if you ask me! Clearly a form of self-mutilation. In fact, though I'm not a psychologist, I would say this is a big warning sign.

Since you keep talking about self-mutilation, would you like to add anything about cutting?

Cutting is an activity on the rise, particularly among adolescent girls and some guys. In this situation, the individual takes a knife or razor and cuts her skin in order to bleed. "Cutters" are seldom suicidal; they seek to injure, not kill, themselves. The urge to cut is often brought on by serious stress, like anger or even a high academic workload. Cutters appear to feel the stress drains from their bodies along with the blood.

Obviously, cutting and bleeding has its share of physical dangers; however, it is only a symptom of a greater psychological problem. I don't want to delve into that very deeply here, because this is where you need a professional for help. Briefly, though, self-mutilation of all sorts indicates a deep unhappiness with who you are—be it looks, size, ability to cope with stress, whatever. In my opinion, today's youth are thrown into a cauldron of pressure that's only getting worse. Christians suffer these same troubles. Always, always, always remember who you are—whose you are—and the worth you have in God's eyes: He has given His only Son to redeem you. You are His treasure.

if i'm in high school and stick pencils up my nose, what should i do?

First, carefully remove the pencil. Second, don't do it again.

i did something wrong and i feel really guilty. Do i have to forgive myself before God can forgive me?

First off, thanks be to God you feel guilty! This is proof that (a) you haven't completely dulled your conscience and (b) the Holy Spirit hasn't stopped working to convict you of sin (John 16:8). Guilt is a terrible feeling, but it's a blessing since it persuades you not to go back and do the same thing again.

As far as forgiving yourself, I've had Christians tell me God can't forgive you until you do. But think about it, if you have to forgive yourself before God can forgive you, then you have to do something to be forgiven. But you're not saved by your works: you're saved solely because Jesus did the work of saving you. So instead of trying to forgive yourself before expecting God to forgive, confess your sins—including your inability to forgive yourself! You have God's certain promise that He forgives you.

That's good news, because you're likely to mess up badly enough that you carry regret around for a long time. It's a big comfort, even while you work through the shame, to know that God has already forgiven you— long before your toes stop curling in embarrassment.

i confessed my sin, but i still feel guilty. Am i forgiven?

Yup! The guilt will hang around a while as your conscience keeps working you over. Be careful, though. Sometimes people believe they aren't forgiven until they feel forgiven. In this case, they're saying you earn God's forgiveness by feeling good. The truth is you are already forgiven. God's Word doesn't require your feelings to forgive you.

If you continue to feel guilty, go confess your sin again—not the one you've been forgiven for already, but the sin of doubting God's forgiveness. It's a great comfort to hear the Absolution. God forgives you for this sin, too.

55

Some people laugh at me and call me a perfectionist. i just think you should do things as well as you can. Am i wrong?

I would say no. But then again, I'm usually compelled to alphabetize my sock drawer.

God creates some people with a much greater passion for details and exactness, and that's a blessing. I'd much rather have someone like you designing buildings and bridges than someone who thinks "2+2=5ish" is close enough. The desire for precision is a necessary skill for a lot of important jobs, among them engineering, law, architecture, and theology. As a rule, accuracy is pretty helpful for SAT tests and scholarships, too.

It doesn't hurt your free throw percentage, either.

On the other hand, you can drive yourself (and others) unnecessarily nuts. Some things, like an internal combustion engine or the study of Scripture, need to be done a certain way. Other things, like a proper breakfast or the right route to school, are open to some interpretation. You're going to cause some needless hard feelings when you insist your way is the only way, when it's not. Along those lines, while attention to detail is a gift, so is the ability of others to relax and deal with pressure better. Furthermore, remember that you're living in a sinful, imperfect world. While you should do your best, it's simply unrealistic to expect yourself to be perfect all the time. God doesn't love you because you're perfect. He gave His perfect Son to redeem you from your sinful imperfections.

i hate losing. is this good or bad?

I'm not a big fan of losing either. Especially in the sports world, you hear all sorts of cute sayings like, "Winning isn't everything, it's the only thing" and "No one remembers who came in second place." Blah, blah, blah.

I like winning, but get used to this fact: you're going to lose. Whether it's a spelling test or a baseball game, you might be the champ for a while; but sooner or later, you're going to give up the trophy to somebody who's better than you. Don't decide you're good or bad based on the scoreboard or the trophy case. Your identity comes from God, who gave His Son to conquer death for you: that victory is yours, and it's never going to go away.

Sometimes, when i do something wrong, i don't feel sorry about it. What should i do?

Confess the sin—and confess your lack of sorrow. Even when your mind and body are telling you the sin was good or fun, you know better by God's Word. If it's sin, confess the sin. Sometimes, there's a silly notion you shouldn't confess until you've made yourself feel how sinful you are. Don't rely on your feelings. Trust what God's Word says.

i keep hearing that self-esteem is important, but my pastor doesn't seem to like the term. Any idea why?

In really basic terms, self-esteem is the idea you should feel good about yourself. The better you feel about yourself, the less likely you are to be depressed, or to experiment with drugs or promiscuity. The more likely you are to keep trying to do your best in school, studies, sports, and so forth. That's why people regard self-esteem as an important quality.

I'll confess I'm not the biggest fan of the term because of the word "self." I know my Old Adam (my old sinful nature) all too well. The more I feel good about myself, the less I want to confess I'm a sinner who needs a Savior. That's the danger of self-esteem: in encouraging you to feel good about yourself, it tempts you to deny there's anything wrong with you at all.

So howzabout this? Rather than focus your esteem on *who* you are, make it about *whose* you are. Rather than boast about your skills (pride), rejoice in the talents God has given you (thankfulness). Rather than take credit for who you are—as if you had a big hand in mixing up your DNA, give thanks to God for who He's made you and use those gifts to serve others . . . instead of just yourself.

i want to look as good as i can. is that wrong?

This question could be about either beauty or fitness, so let's look at both.

Like all things, physical beauty is a gift of God. It's okay to be attractive. However, beauty has its share of temptations in a sinful world. If you're good-looking, you're going to want to use your looks for attention and to get the advantage over others. You're going to be tempted to believe you're better because you're beautiful—once again, as if you had anything to do with your looks. The desire to be/stay beautiful may lead you to eating disorders like anorexia and bulimia. Furthermore, be aware that as you attract people, you're going to attract some incredible losers who want to spend time with you for all the wrong reasons.

Likewise, it's not wrong to be athletic or physically fit. Athletic talent is also a gift of God. But in this sinful world, athleticism and fitness also have their share of temptations. If you're athletic, you're going to be tempted to make an idol out of your fitness and the popularity it brings. You might be tempted to ignore studies, church, and other important matters to hang around the gym all the time, leaving you an athletic, irreligious ignoramus. There's nothing worse than a conversation with a 40-year-old guy who can only talk about how good a shooting guard he was in high school, because he never studied to do anything with his life. You might even be tempted to break the law and use steroids for cheap bulk now, even though they can disfigure or kill you.

It's not wrong to be beautiful or athletic. These are gifts of God. But while they're showy gifts, they're fleeting—you're not going to beautiful or physically fit for all of your life, so don't put your trust in these things. Instead, use them in service to others, not for your own vanity and gain.

59

i don't look good and i'm not a jock. Why did God do this to me?

Our society puts a big emphasis on beauty and fitness. It worships beauty and fitness. For some reason, I'm still waiting for Nike or Adidas to use me in an ad campaign. Come to think of it, no one's asked me to model clothing for them, either. Maybe I need an agent. But back to your question.

I'm guessing you look better than you think you

do, since we sinfully tend to (a) be critical of our looks and resent who God has made us to be, and (b) envy the looks that others have. Even so, if you're not exceptionally stunning or athletic, it's okay: you won't face a lot of the temptations I mentioned in the previous question. You'll face others, but not those. Furthermore, there are a lot greater gifts in this world than beauty and fitness, for use in service to others: gifts like intelligence, compassion, repentance, and more. Whether you're male or female, remember Proverbs 31:30: "Charm is deceitful, and beauty is vain, but a woman who fears the Lord is to be praised." The same goes for a man who fears the Lord. God gave His Son to die for you, to cleanse you and redeem you. In Christ, you're His beautiful child.

60

i want to serve God, but i'm so busy between school and chores at home. How can i serve Him?

You're going to love this answer—by going to school and doing your chores at home. Sometimes along the way, we get this idea that you only serve God when you're doing something extraordinary—like you go to Peru on spring break to build a school or something. Plug in some common sense here: if this is true, it means you're only serving God for very small bits of your life.

Remember, God works through our stations in life. Your station is where you ordinarily are. If you make it to Peru, that's just fine. But on every other day, if you have the station of "son" or "daughter," your service to God is to honor your parents, like the Fourth Commandment says. If your station is "student," then your service to God is to study, do your homework and honor your teacher.

Oh, and don't forget the greatest worship of God is, by the Holy Spirit's work, to make use of the forgiveness Jesus won for you. Jesus said, "For this is the will of My Father, that everyone who looks on the Son and believes in Him should have eternal life, and I will raise him up on the last day" (John 6:40). As you daily remember your Baptism and repent; as you confess your sins and receive forgiveness; as you hear the Word and receive Holy Communion; God delights—for the forgiveness you receive in these means of grace is what Jesus died to give you.

62 Section 3:
Parents
and Other
Authorities

Unless you are currently being raised by a pack of wolves, you're being raised by *a* parent, parents, grandparents, or other guardians who have authority over you. For the sake of this discussion, we'll call them "parents," since that's their station. You may or may not be getting along with your parents all that well right now. But whether or not you do, God gave you the Fourth Commandment: "Honor your father and your mother, that your days may be long in the land that the LORD your God is giving you" (Exodus 20:12). This commandment is worth exploring in a bit of detail, as we look at service, station, sin, and the solution.

"Honor . . ." While God commands you to love your neighbor, He commands you to honor your parents. This means that you owe them not just love, but obedience, humility and dutiful service. That's the service God emphasizes when your station is "son" or "daughter."

"Your father and your mother . . ." In the last chapter, we noted the greatest treasures receive the least amount of praise in this world. Back in chapter 1, we saw that everyone is given their station in life to serve. **63** These two teachings are never more true than with parents. Parents are given authority over their children in order to serve them. When you were born, you were a cute little blob who couldn't do anything for yourself—your parents had to do it all. While you were growing up, you had to be taught to eat your vegetables, tie your shoes, and not draw on the walls with permanent markers. On the days you were a pain and wanted only to defy them, they did not have the option of returning you to the baby store under warranty. As you get ready to leave your teen years, it gets even trickier. While your parents are still raising you as their kid, they also need to train you to be independent from them. This situation creates a bit of friction. Sometimes, you'll want to be independent faster than they're willing. Other times, you'll want their help while they want you on your own.

My point so far is: parents are servants who do a lot of serving. Just as you are commanded to honor them, they are commanded to act in a way worthy of honor (see Ephesians 6:4). There really are things your parents would rather have done than clean your diaper (seriously, is there a humbler job than wiping someone else's bottom?) or spend hours teaching you to tie your shoes. Give them a break. No, give them honor. That's what God tells you to do.

Your parents can't do it all, so they enlist others to help. Because they aren't skilled in every area, and because they have to make a living, they often put you in the care of educators. In other words, they send you **64** to school. At school, you are to honor your teachers— why? Because they're teaching you on behalf of your parents, who have shared their authority with them. When you honor your teachers, you honor your parents. When you honor your parents, you keep the Fourth Commandment.

It doesn't stop there. Luther says so. Many moons ago, most businesses were conducted in homes, mansions, estates, and the like. The head of the house had servants who did the work of the business. To the servants, the boss was known as the "house-father." Guess what? The house-father deserved honor.

While you may not have an after-school job in a home business, in whatever job you have, the Lord calls you to honor your boss.

> Slaves, obey your earthly masters with fear and trembling, with a sincere heart, as you would Christ, not by the way of eye-service, as people-pleasers, but as servants of Christ, doing the will of God from the heart, rendering service with a good will as to the Lord and not to man, knowing that whatever good anyone does, this he will receive back from the Lord, whether he is a slave or free. **(Ephesians 6:5–8)**

When you honor your boss and do your work, you honor the Lord.

It doesn't stop there, either. In the Large Catechism, Luther called rulers the "fathers of the country," since they are placed by God to serve and protect the citizens entrusted to their care. This means you also owe honor to the police officer who pulls you over, the mayor, the president, and others. Luther didn't pull this out of thin air, he read it in Romans 13:1–7.

All of this is included in the Fourth Commandment, so rejoice! Look at all the ways you have to serve God and do His will! When you obey your parents and clean up your room or get home by curfew, you're keeping the Fourth Commandment and doing what God wants you to do. When you get your homework done and pay attention in class, you're keeping the Fourth Commandment and doing God's will. When you thank the officer for telling you to slow down . . . well, you get the idea.

65

"That your days may be long in the land that the Lord your God is giving you." When St. Paul repeats the Fourth Commandment in Ephesians 6:2–3, he's quick to point out that "this is the first commandment with a promise." This is a common sense, cause-and-effect sort of promise, because a promise of the Law is based upon your efforts. So, if you learn to honor your parents, then you've learned to honor your teachers. If you don't . . .

Sin is always lurking in this station. Conceived in sin, selfish people like you and me don't want to honor authorities: we want to do what we darn well please. This disobedience dishonors your parents and God who gave them to you, all of which deserves eternal judgment. Along the way, there are some practical consequences. If you don't honor your parents, you won't honor your teachers. If you don't learn to honor your teachers, then you don't get an education and you have less opportunity to make an honest living. You might get a job, but you've never learned to honor authorities so you mouth off to your employer and get fired. This leaves you to make a dishonest living. If you're living by crime, you're not honoring the authorities, who will eventually track you down and put you in the slammer, or—as Luther so kindly puts it—give you a date with the hangman. The more you break this commandment, the more likely it is that you won't have a long, happy life. And no matter how hard you try, you'll never keep it perfectly.

Now, here's the solution—the Good News before we move on—Jesus was the perfect child. He grew up

66

honoring His foster father and mother in Nazareth (Luke 2:51), and also pleased His heavenly Father by doing His will (Luke 3:22; Matthew 26:42). In honoring His Father, He went to the cross and died for your sins—including all the times you haven't honored your parents and other authorities. Therefore, Christ forgives you for these and all of your sins. And while the promise of the Fourth Commandment isn't certain, His promise of forgiveness is.

That should be enough to get us started, so . . .

Q & A:
You Ask . .

68

is it wrong to question authority?

No. The Lord doesn't tell you to obey authorities blindly, because authorities are sinful, too. If authorities are misled enough, they may try to lead you into sin. Part of growing up is learning to evaluate the wisdom of others, including authorities. You're not commanded to be a mindless robot. You are, however, to honor authorities—even when they make a mistake. Some of the following questions will offer examples.

My curfew is just unfair.
How do i deal with my parents on this?

Make sure you whine and complain a lot. Then stay out two hours late to prove just how responsible and trustworthy you are.

Or, think again. Whether or not your curfew is unfair is your opinion—I just can't find a Bible verse or scientific law about how late kids can stay out. You have your opinion, and your parents have theirs. According to the Fourth Commandment, your opinion isn't necessarily wrong but you have the responsibility to honor Mom and Dad. To deal with this, honor the curfew. You can, if you want, make a respectful argument about why you think you deserve a later time. As you gain more trust, you'll get more freedom.

69

My parents won't let me do something, when i know for a fact that they used to sneak around and do it when they were my age. is that hypocritical or what?

Hmmm . . . I'm going to go with "or what." If "it" involves "sneaking around," this tells me that "it's" not the best thing to be doing—quite possibly not the most healthy or legal, either. I don't care if it looks fun. Fun does not equal good or godly.

So you say your parents used to do whatever, and now they won't let you do it. It could be they've made it their goal in life to deprive you of all meaningful entertainment. Or, just maybe, they love you and don't want you to do the same stupid things and make the same stupid mistakes they did. By now, you can look back at less than smart things you've done, like jumping off the sofa onto the lamp and nearly setting the cat on fire. As you look back, you think, "I'll never do that again." That's called common sense, fueled by hindsight. Your parents look back at their lives and think, "That was pretty foolish. Let's try to make sure our kids aren't quite as idiotic as we were, so they have fewer regrets and injuries."

This is not hypocrisy. It's only hypocrisy if your parents are still jumping off the sofa into lamps and setting the cat on fire. If they are trying to prevent you from the sins of their youth, then it's love, informed by common sense and hard knocks.

70

My parents don't trust me on the internet. i have to get permission to go to any Web site, they even installed software to monitor everything i do. Why don't they trust me?

First, let's talk about the Internet. It's full of all sorts of useful information, from statistics I can use in a book like this to how to fix my water softener in the basement. The worldwide Web is weally cool. Of course, the Internet is also full of porn sites, wicked chat rooms, and sexual predators masquerading as fifteen-year-olds. If your parents are aware, then you can expect some regulation. They're trying to keep you safe; they know your weaknesses. They also know they can't be sitting next to you all the time.

Second, let's talk about trust. Trust must be earned. If you've done something to violate your parents' trust in you, then you're going to have to work hard to get it back. If you have a history of going to crummy Web sites, then you're paying the consequences for your poor judgment. While your personal safety is one issue, so is honesty and trust. Before your parents trust you with bigger things, they need to be able to trust you with smaller things.

Honor your parents, follow the rules and earn their trust. Greater privileges will follow.

i want to go to a party, but Mom and Dad said no. My best friends' parents said it was okay for them to go, but my parents still said no. What do you think?

71

Like it or not, your parents have the station of raising you. Your friends' parents have the station of raising your friends. Therefore, guess who you get to honor first in your station? Your parents, not your friends' parents. That's what the Fourth Commandment says.

Common sense doesn't help you out here either, as in the old mom question, "If all your friends and their parents jumped off a cliff, would you jump off, too?"

My friends love me more than my parents. What do i do?

While what you say is possible, it's not very likely. I'd encourage you to think about stations and love. Your parents have the station of serving you by training you for adulthood. Since that training involves discipline when you make a mistake, you're not always going to get along with them. Your friends, as we'll discuss later, have the vague station of getting along with you, which means you're probably going to get along with them as long as they're your friends.

As far as love goes, your parents probably love you in a sacrificial way. They always take care of you, even when you're unkind enough as to suggest they don't love you at all. On the other hand, your friends usually *love* you as long as you're not doing anything to tick them off.

Friends might appear to love you more; but your parents' station is a lot more committed. Their love runs a whole lot deeper.

Are parents always right?

Nope! They're sinful, too. They don't always express themselves well or communicate clearly, and they certainly can't read minds. They can get cranky and irritable and angry for no good reason. A long time ago, I realized that I couldn't model perfection for my kids. A lot of days, I end up modeling *confession* when I ask them for forgiveness for some grouchy thing I did.

So, yes, sometimes parents can go overboard in making rules too stringent. Sometimes, they might expose you to more trouble than they intended.

Sometimes, it gets a whole lot worse. Enslaved in sin, some parents end up abusing their children physically, sexually, and/or psychologically.

So is it ever okay to disobey my parents?

Acts 5:29 declares, "We must obey God rather than men." Should your parents—or other authorities—command you to do something that disobeys God's Word, then you've got to say no. To do otherwise would be to make them an idol rather than "fear, love and trust in God above all things" (Small Catechism, Explanation to the First Commandment). Honestly, I can't think of a whole lot of situations where parents command their children to disobey God: only a couple come to mind.

73

For one, I think of a young Japanese man whom I met in Tokyo when I was on a choir tour in college. By the grace of God, he believed in Jesus. While he still lived at home, his parents—strict Buddhists—refused to speak to him because of his faith. Still, he was standing firm in confessing Jesus and praying for his parents. I come across similar situations, every now and then, in the United States.

For another, there's the matter of abuse. When a parent is inflicting ongoing physical harm or forcing sexual relations on a child. These victims live in a terribly confused situation, since they're being violated by someone they're supposed to trust. Some may even wonder if it breaks the Fourth Commandment to report the abuse to a teacher, pastor, or the police.

So here's the answer: it's vital to report such abuse! In most cases the abuser has abandoned his or her station as a parent, because this person is no longer serving the child for the child's good. The abuser must be punished for the good of their soul, lest they never repent of their sin and potentially move on to hurt others. Finally, the abuser risks damaging the entire future life of their victim, the victim owes it to his or her future children to try to be as undamaged as possible.

74 Once i'm out of the house, do i still have to honor my parents?

Yes, although the relationship changes. You'll have your own household and your own rules, but you still owe a lot to your parents. Honor them by staying in touch so they don't worry so much. When you find out they were right about something and helped you prepare for life, you might want to let them know. But more to the point is this: your parents took care of you when you were young and weak and helpless. As they grow older, they'll grow weaker and need more help. It's up to you to honor your parents by making sure they're taken care of in their old age.

My parents got a divorce, so i'm from a broken home. Can you talk about that a little?

Sure. While the world does its best to make divorce sound like no big thing, it causes a ton of pain. Remember what we talked about in chapter one? God gives people stations in which to serve one another, while sin seeks to isolate them. Divorce is a prime, painful example.

Marriage is a station in which a man and a woman promise to be servants to one another for life. When I talk to couples who are thinking of marriage, I tell them the *love* required for marriage is a synonym for *hard work*—the hard work of selflessly putting the other person first all the time. The more a husband and wife serve each other, the stronger a marriage is going to be.

75

A divorce happens because one or both persons don't want to serve the other anymore. Sometimes, it's a sudden, gut-wrenching end, like when a husband or wife decides they'd rather serve their own selfish passions by having an affair. Sometimes, it's a gradual thing, where one or both parties pursue their own interests apart from the other. Eventually they decide they just don't have any common interests and want to go in different directions. These failures to serve are sinful, and sin works to isolate. Divorce ends up isolating people and leaving them angry, confused, and grief-stricken. This doesn't just apply to the couple. If they have kids, it applies to them, too.

When parents divorce, it usually means shared custody. Kids spend weeks with Mom and weekends with Dad or some similar arrangement. It's important for kids to spend time with each parent, but here's a problem: one parent can't raise kids as well as two. A single parent has to worry about all the adult responsibilities (paying bills, planning meals, etc.), so they carry twice the load of work at home; this also means they have less time to interact with their kids. Sometimes, when it gets really ugly, divorced parents try to turn the kids against the other parent. One parent will spoil them when they visit, leaving the other to handle all the discipline and look like the bad guy.

So if i'm from a broken home, how does all this affect me?

First off, it's not your fault. Children often blame themselves for the actions of their parents, because they believe they've caused the split. (It really doesn't help that, in months before a divorce, the adults are really high-strung and tend to snap at their kids a lot, making the kids wonder what they keep doing wrong.) If your parents have divorced, it's not your fault. They made the vows, and they broke them. I'll save the rest of that speech for them sometime.

Remember one of our standing rules in this book is that life isn't fair. Even though it's not your fault, you're still going to suffer the consequences of a parental decision. While there's nothing you and I can do to make life more fair, it's helpful for you to know some of the specific temptations you face.

A very present temptation is the sin of pitting one parent against another. Parents feel terribly guilty for the pain their children suffer during divorce and want to make it up to them. Some kids use this guilt for self-ish gain, "Mom, why do we have to go to bed now? When we're at Dad's, he lets us stay up as long as we want." Or, "Why can't we watch that DVD, Dad? Mom said we could watch it at her house." You'll be tempted to use guilt and pit your parents against each other. Don't do it. When you do, you're giving in to selfishness, manipulating your parents for your own gain.

Another danger is that, with only one adult in the household, you're likely to have a lot of unsupervised time. It's really easy to get into trouble when you're on your own. Kids from broken homes are especially tempted by alcohol, drugs, and promiscuity for a number of reasons. They may abuse substances to escape the feelings of depression. They may turn to promiscuity because sexual contact makes them feel less lonely. They may even get involved in these things as a way of hurting their parents.

The devil is vicious on kids in your situation, tempting you to believe you deserve to indulge in harmful things because you've been hurt so badly. Don't believe it! Whether or not you've been hurt deeply, substance abuse will still addict you and put your life in danger. Whether or not you come from a broken home, promiscuity still offers disease, a greater chance at failed relationships later, maybe even death.

These are ways not to live long on the earth.

The sum of all this advice and law is this: even though it's not your fault, do your best to live at all times like you're not a victim. Don't buy into the temptation of believing that all sorts of sins are okay because you've suffered.

Of course, this is really easy for me to say and really difficult for you to do. This is deep hurt we're talking about, and you're going to find yourself angry and grief-stricken, thinking all sorts of evil thoughts and tempted to do all sorts of things. That's why, ultimately, the best thing I can do is point you back to the cross and your Savior. On the cross, Jesus was the victim of all sin as God punished Him for *all transgressions* of *all people* for *all time*. On Calvary, the scourge and nails and cross, as hideously painful as they were, were nothing like the agony Jesus suffered as the sacrifice for all sin. But He suffered and died this hideous death for you and for your parents. He has forgiveness for them and for you. And while you live in a world so messed up by sin that even parents prove less than faithful, Jesus has already proved Himself faithful to you unto death. And risen again, He will never leave you nor forsake you.

if i'm from a broken home, does this have an effect on future relationships and marriage for me?

Yes! It's good to keep the big picture in mind. For one thing, in God's plan of an intact family, kids get to see an example of marriage where husband and wife work hard to serve each other. This daily service teaches kids how to build a strong marriage. If you live in a broken home, you're deprived of this example. You may be seeing two single parents who have only themselves to rely on, who work very hard just to take care of themselves. Self-sufficiency is a good trait—but it doesn't teach you how to serve someone else. This may seem silly to say at this point in your life, but keep in mind that someday you'll probably be married. Since you haven't learned the importance of serving your spouse by the example of your parents, it's going to be more of a challenge for you. Instead, you've learned not to fully commit to another, lest you get burned. If you've spent time manipulating your parents, then you've trained yourself to manipulate your spouse, too. You've also been taught, unintentionally, that marriage vows really aren't "'til death do us part," so you'll want to make sure you're ready to commit to a lifetime relationship yourself. In fact, it would do you good to read a bunch of books on the subject, maybe even speak with a trained counselor. You can work through all this and have a strong, successful loving marriage. Remember—it's all about serving.

79

Here's another thing to watch out for in the future, as bizarre as it sounds right now. You might have heard the old saying that guys marry women who are like their moms while girls marry men who are like their dads. It sounds odd—but think it through—when things go according to God's plan, a father models the qualities of a good husband to his wife for his daughter, so the daughter learns what qualities to look for in a guy. However, even when parents don't model good qualities, sons and daughters both tend to be attracted to mates who resemble their parents. It won't be easy when you're in love, but step back and see if a potential spouse has the same reluctance to serve that hurt your parents' marriage.

My divorced parents have shared custody, and each has different rules for me. What do i do?

You still honor your parents. Honor your father's rules at his house and your mother's rules at hers. Even though they may have really messed up, they're in deep pain. Do your best to serve them and help them out.

Do i have to honor my stepparents?

Yes, because your biological parents brought them into the household as husband or wife. I admit, this can be really difficult, since you'll often see a stepparent as someone who's keeping your parents apart permanently. So plug in a little common sense: is it going to help out the situation if you treat stepparents with open hostility? Nope! Try to serve, honor and forgive. Remember the Lord's service and forgiveness for you.

80

You pointed out Ephesians 6:1–3, where the Bible says the Fourth Commandment comes with a promise, "that it may go well with you and that you may live long in the land." But a lot of young, "good" people seem to die: they get cancer or get in a car accident or something. Does this mean God doesn't keep this promise?

No! God always keeps His promises. In this case, however, the promise is built upon a commandment, something we are supposed to do. Therefore, it depends upon the behavior of people—sinful people— you and me included. God doesn't break this promise. People destroy life by their sin.

You don't live in a bubble on your own. You live in a world with a bunch of sinful people—and the fulfillment of this promise depends on their behavior, too. I can do my best to honor authorities and live an obedient life, but that doesn't prevent somebody else from driving while drunk and killing me. I can do my best to pick a safe spot to live, but that doesn't prevent someone else from burying some cancer-causing substance in the ground that will eventually do me in. When other people break the law, they hurt others, too.

This is why the Gospel is so wonderful. Forgiveness and salvation depend on Jesus and His work, not us and our obedience. I *can't* be sure that I'm going to live to see tomorrow, because this is a danger-

81

ous world where my mistakes or someone else's might kill me. I *can* be sure I'm going to live forever, because Jesus never makes a mistake and always keeps His promises.

My teacher is soooooooo boring. Do i have to honor him?

First off, make sure you examine yourself. We live in an entertainment age: between television, satellite radio, MP3s, and more, you and I can find something to titillate our minds at any time. This has a dangerous effect: you start to think you have to be entertained in order to pay attention. If you find someone boring, it may not be their fault at all. It may be you have a short attention span, while you're blaming others for your problems.

That said, everybody has a different personality, and some people are going to be more exciting than others. This applies to teachers, too. While it's easier to learn from someone who is engaging, you learn from anyone who has information to give you—even if they do it in a less-than-exciting manner. God doesn't tell you to honor only those who aren't boring. He tells you to honor those who are in authority. This also gives you an excellent opportunity to work on self-control, to discipline yourself to learn without being entertained. Believe me, this is an important skill. There are a lot of boring people out there.

My teacher makes it clear that she doesn't believe in God and pokes fun at religion. How can i honor her when she's doing this?

It's always easier to honor authorities when they're doing their best to honor God, but that's often not the case. In the case of your teacher, your station as student requires you to honor her by listening, studying, getting the homework done, and not being disruptive. You're not required to agree with a teacher's opinions. Set a good example of honoring her; it's not going to help the situation on any level if you rebel against your teacher in the name of Jesus.

83

So is it okay to disagree with a teacher?

It's okay to disagree about an opinion. Just do it in a respectful manner, not something like, "Any numbskull would say you're wrong." Be polite and present a good argument for your side. Most teachers I've met appreciate a student who thinks about an issue enough to make a good case, even if it dissents from their viewpoint.

On the other hand, I wouldn't be contradicting teachers on their teaching style or classroom management plan. Why? Because that belongs to other people with other stations—like principals and your parents.

i've got an after-school job, and i'm having a tough time with my boss. Any advice?

Bosses are natural targets for complaints; but before you go there, let's analyze the situation a little. Your boss has the station of supervising you. It's his responsibility to serve the customers by providing them with what they need. He's also to serve his employer/company by making a decent profit and establishing a good reputation. And, of course, he's also to serve you—how? By making sure you're properly trained for your job and safe while you're doing it.

As an employee, it's your job to serve the customer and to honor your boss by doing the best job you can.

Remember, your boss has a sinful nature, and so do you. So why are you having a tough time with your boss?

It could be that he's unfair or that he's just not a nice guy. It could be he's got some problems with discrimination because of your gender or race. It could be he's under a lot of pressure and just about to explode, so he's going to snap at anyone who can't snap back. Truthfully, there are some pretty crummy bosses out there.

Or, it could be that it's you. Employees have been known for doing the bare minimum, rather than putting a lot of effort into their work. I've heard people complain about their bosses because they weren't allowed to do their homework while they were on the job, or because they couldn't get time off every time they wanted it. If you're not doing your part, don't expect your boss to cut you a lot of slack.

It could also be somewhere in between, where both of you aren't quite operating the way you should.

What to do? Clearly, if your boss is telling you to break the law, act immorally or put yourself in danger, quit now. Otherwise, I would counsel you to do your best at whatever job you have—this helps the boss get his job done and eases the tension between the two of you. If you have a suggestion about the company, make it respectfully; and if he doesn't go for it, just go back to work. If things are just awful, find a trustworthy adult and talk about the situation to see if you need to make some changes. If conditions remain horrible, you can always get another job. One of the luxuries of high school is that jobs can be pretty easy to find.

85

it's okay to make fun of elected officials when they make fools of themselves, right?

It's easy, but I wouldn't say it's okay. Officials have authority in part because they're elected by "we, the people"; however, they wouldn't have gotten elected if the Lord hadn't allowed them the position. So when you ridicule an official, you're ridiculing someone whom God has put in place (Romans 13:4). Even if they've done something that makes them a prime and easy target—I could write satire after satire about government officials—it's not a good thing to do.

Consider Jesus as He stood on trial before Pontius

Pilate. For reasons too many to list here, Pilate was a terrible ruler long before Good Friday. In the case of Jesus, Pilate did such a horrible job he declared Jesus completely innocent three times—and then had the innocent man scourged and crucified! Somewhere on the way, integrity and competence passed Pilate by.

Even so, what did Jesus say to Pilate during His trial? Jesus answered him, "You would have no authority over me at all unless it had been given you from above. Therefore he who delivered Me over to you has the greater sin" (John 19:11). Even though Pilate was doing a horrible job and putting an innocent man to death, Jesus still honored Pilate's station— even though Jesus had given him the authority in the first place!

86

On television, the news showed a pastor who was telling people they shouldn't pay taxes because the government sponsors abortion. is he right?

This is a tough question. Certainly, you and I don't want to use our money to support sinful practices, and there's no doubt abortion is a sin. On the other hand, the Roman Empire wasn't exactly the most godly kingdom in Jesus' time. To keep order and suppress rebellion, they committed all sorts of atrocities. So one day, the Pharisees and Herodians confronted Jesus with this very question, "Is it lawful to pay taxes to Caesar, or not? Should we pay them, or should we not?" (Mark 12:14). Jesus told them, "Render to Caesar the things that are Caesar's, and to God the things that are God's" (Mark 12:17). Even though Caesar was far from a godly ruler and tax money would be used to finance all sorts of sin, Jesus still told people to pay their taxes.

Can God use non-Christians as rulers to get His will accomplished?

Yes, He can and He does. After the people of Judah were taken into captivity to Babylon, the Lord used Cyrus, King of Persia, to get them back to Jerusalem. Scholars think Cyrus might have had a little knowledge of their religion, but there's no proof he was a believer. Nevertheless, God said of him, "He is My shepherd, and he shall fulfill all My purpose" (Isaiah 44:28). Remember the Lord is all-powerful: He doesn't need our help or our trust in order to get His work done. However, He rejoices to use us as His instruments. What a privilege we have!

if i disagree with an elected official, how can i express my opinion and still honor him?

In most of history, you didn't have a lot of ways to disagree except to say no and suffer. In democratic countries today, you have the great privilege of expressing your views by voting. As soon as you are old enough, please study the issues and candidates carefully and then participate in elections! Even if you're not old enough, you can write to elected officials and voice your disagreement—just do so in a respectful manner.

Should i honor a Christian authority more than a non-Christian authority?

No, the Lord would have you honor both:

> First of all, then, I urge that supplications, prayers, intercessions, and thanksgivings be made for all people, for kings and all who are in high positions, that we may lead a peaceful and quiet life, godly and dignified in every way. This is good, and it is pleasing in the sight of God our Savior, who desires all people to be saved and to come to the knowledge of the truth.
> (1 Timothy 2:1–4)

I'll add a couple words of caution about "Christian" rulers. One is that many who run for office in the United States will call themselves Christian, even if they don't especially believe in Christ. They may simply mean they share the same basic morals as many Christian churches. The other is being a Christian and being competent are not the same thing. An individual who is a sincere believer may be train wreck in office if he doesn't have the skills to get the job done. A non-Christian, however, may have the values and skills to be an excellent official. That's life in the real world.

For more questions dealing with parents in family matters, see the next chapter dealing with siblings.

All in all, authorities are a gift of God, given by Him to keep order in this world. That is a blessing, and necessary. When you encounter friction with someone in authority, it's either because you want to do something that doesn't honor them, or they want to do something that doesn't honor God. In the first case, repent. In the second, honor the Lord and do your best to respect the one in charge. Not every authority is going to be the best. Some are going to treat you pretty poorly. That's how life goes in this sinful world. So always remember—the final authority is Jesus Christ, King of kings and Lord of lords (Revelation 19:16). No matter how other authorities treat you, know this for sure—when you stand before the final authority on Judgment Day, forgiven for all of your sin, the Judge will say, "Well done, O good and faithful servant. Heaven is yours."

90 # Section Four: Siblings

Since the average American family still produces more than one child apiece, chances are you have a brother or sister. You may greet this news with joy or sadness, depending on how well you get along with your siblings, or what's happened in your house in the last five minutes. Indeed, the old saying holds true; you can pick your friends, but you can't pick your family. And you ought not pick your nose.

The Bible doesn't say much specifically about how siblings should treat each other. Of course the Bible contains stories concerning siblings. Rivalry between the first two brothers, resulted in Cain killing Abel (Genesis 4:8). Don't do that! Joseph's brothers sold him into slavery (Genesis 37:28). Don't do that, either! Mary and Martha had squabbles over chores, though Jesus' answer surprises a lot of people (Luke 10:38–42). The Bible is full of stories about siblings who didn't get along. I suppose I could write some really helpful advice like, "If you have eleven brothers who positively hate you, don't go out in a field alone with them and a bunch of slave traders," but you don't really need the Bible to tell you that. If you have any common sense at all, you know better already. Since, however, there's no chapter in the Bible entitled, "Dealing with your little brother," we'd better approach this from a different angle.

91

What defines your relationship? It's not that the two of you think the same, act the same or may remotely be the same. After all, you're different ages unless you're twins. And while four year's difference isn't a big deal to people in their thirties, a newborn baby and her five-year-old brother look like different life-forms. There's still a huge difference in maturity between a nine-year-old brother and a thirteen-year-old sister. In some cases, there may be more than a ten-year gap between two siblings, which will make their relationship different. It will feel more like a parent-child than sibling relationship.

Furthermore, you might not be the same sex, and—brace yourself, because someone has to tell you some-time—boys and girls are not the same. You may never figure out why your brother or sister acts the way they do.

Even if you're the same sex, you are different people. Birth order seems to play into this equation. The first child often imitates the parents, while the second distinguishes himself by not imitating parents. The third, I'm told, is often more easygoing than the first two. Whether it's the way the DNA got put together or different circumstances in life, you are different from even your closest sibling.

The differences between you and your siblings can be good or bad. Your differences may complement each other, so you can help each other out. On the other hand, you're both sinful and prone to sins like jealousy and covetousness. Therefore, you might resent the talents the other has or the awards they receive.

92

Having said this, it's tough to write stuff that applies to all sibling relationships. Your relationship with brothers or sisters may be somewhat like good friends, distant cousins, or even uneasy coworkers who are under the same roof with little else in common. It's really tough to describe your station as a brother or sister. However, some basic truths should be taken to heart. Before the questions about this station, we emphasize a couple of things—like service . . .

1. Once again, there's a lot to be said for forgiveness and service to one another.

This is not easy, since you grow up with Old Adam teaching you your siblings are your greatest rivals—for soccer skills, Mom's attention, good grades, or whatever. Competitiveness can be a great motivator . . . or it can turn you into enemies. If you are going to live under the same roof for eighteen years or more, you don't want to be enemies. That's where forgiveness comes in—as in you asking forgiveness when you're wrong, and forgiving others when they've messed up. Furthermore, part of growing up is learning to let others go first. Go to your little brother's soccer game. Congratulate your sister on her report card. Where your siblings excel and show talent you don't have, give thanks to God that He made them the way they are. After all, you don't want a bunch of untalented, low-motivation siblings coming to you for money when you're all grown up, do you? Forgive one another. Serve one another.

93

2. Serving equals love.

The more you serve someone, the more you love them. Eighteen years under the same roof is a lot of time for serving. That's why you will probably end up with a pretty strong loyalty to your siblings, even if you don't have much in common with them.

3. There's a lot to be said for family loyalty.

Here's why: as they say, the family is the basic building block of society. This is simply common sense. In strong families, parents work together and spend time with their kids to train them how to be responsible people, faithful Christians, loving servants, and good citizens. A community is strong when its people are responsible citizens who serve one another. When this doesn't happen in the family, the kids miss out on the training. All too easily, they're no longer responsible citizens, but selfish types living by Old Adam's temptations. When everyone in the community is living only for themselves, the community is bound to be in bad shape. When the family is strong, the community is strong.

Sometimes, a family is weakened by events beyond their control, like a tragic accident. Sometimes, it's the actions of parents that lead to divorce and a broken family. As a son/brother or daughter/sister, you're affected. When you live in the same house with someone, you get to know them really well. While other people only see their best side, you see it all. The rest of your family sees most of you, too. If you want to weaken your family and make your household an awful place to live, start going around blabbing all the bad habits and mistakes of your parents and siblings. Shame and anger will come back at you in waves. Worse, start telling lies to make others look bad, so you can't be trusted anymore. Psalm 50:20 lists this as an evil which ranks up there with adultery. Far better is to help keep the family strong by keeping private stuff within the family. Proverbs 19:11 offers some divinely inspired common sense, "Good sense makes one slow to anger, and it is his glory to overlook an offense." Keep family matters in the family.

4. There are limits to family loyalty.

You need to honor authority. Sin is still sin, even when it's someone within your family who is guilty. Sometimes, you'll get the idea you need to help a brother or sister conceal sin, but remember you are to honor God first. What's the goal of concealing sin? To get away with it, not to confess and be forgiven.

Now, while I'm thinking of crimes like breaking the lamp in the basement, it can be a whole lot more serious. Back in Deuteronomy 13:6–10, the Lord warned that He required obedience first to Himself, not to family. If a brother sought to lure you to other gods, "you shall not yield to him or listen to him, nor shall your eye pity him" (Deuteronomy 13:8). Later, Jesus warned that the temptation to honor family over God was still real, and a sin that would lead to tragedy, "Brother will deliver brother over to death, and the father his child, and children will rise against parents and have them put to death" (Matthew 10:21).

Family loyalty has its limits. Why? If nothing else, every member of your family has sin in common. You're all sinful. That means you are tempted to do the wrong thing, and you'll be tempted to ask others in the family to help. This means something else—you all

95

need a Savior.

That's why God demands loyalty to Himself above all else, as in "You shall have no other gods before Me" (Exodus 20:3). It's not that God needs and can't live without your love. He's been doing quite well on His own from eternity. Rather, you can't live without His love—the love He freely offers to you in Christ Jesus (Romans 3:24).

Even if your closest sibling should let you down, remember Jesus' words: "For whoever does the will of My Father in heaven is My brother and sister and mother." (Matthew 12:50). That's you. Because He forgives you, Jesus declares you His brother. He's also loyal. He already went to the cross and died for you. He remains the solution, your Savior. Risen again, He won't leave you or forsake you.

96

Q&A:
You Ask . . .

97

My brother has some disabilities, so he gets a lot more attention from my parents than i do. is that fair?

It's not fair in all sorts of ways. It's certainly not fair for your brother to have some disabilities, since he'll have difficulty with all sorts of things we take for granted. And no, it isn't fair that you get less attention from your parents because of it. Remember in this broken, sin-filled world, life isn't fair.

When one child is sick or disabled, he gets more attention than the other kids because he needs more help. It doesn't mean the parents love him more;

rather, it means he requires more attention. The fact you can do a lot of things for yourself is a blessing, and it's one your parents appreciate probably more than you know.

Growing up in a household with someone who's disabled can cause a lot of exhaustion and stress, so I plead with you to remember the Lord's will is for all to serve one another. In addition to taking care of yourself, I would encourage you to do your best to help out your brother as much as you can. This will strengthen your love for one another, which will help weaken the resentment both of you feel for your situations. This will also help ease the load on your parents, a great service to them.

98 Why does my brother always have to be better than me?

It's called sibling rivalry; and honestly, it wouldn't bother you so much if you didn't want to be better than him. Siblings want to outdo each other. They want to run faster, score more goals, get better grades, or get more praise.

Is this a good thing? It has some uses to it. Human beings can be pretty lazy, so sibling rivalry teaches the two of you a healthy competition. Careful, though, you can spend a lot of time being jealous your brother is better, or resentful you don't have the same skills. Some of this is just crazy, like when a three-year-old gets mad that he can't run as fast as an eight-year-old. Above and beyond sibling rivalry, be sure to give thanks God made you the way you are and your brother the way he is.

My sister is so much prettier than i am that you'd never know we were sisters. Why did God do this to me?

This is a tough question to answer without knowing a lot more information. Without knowing you personally, my first hunch is you are your own worst critic, actually far from ugly. Even so, I understand this can be a difficult situation. Our society puts a huge emphasis on external beauty and popularity. It's easy to be jealous of who your sister is and who you're not. Looks are a big issue in high school.

But here's the thing. In His divine wisdom, God made you different from your sister. Beauty is one of His gifts, but He gives lots of others, too. He's given those gifts to you. Those who have extremely attractive looks deal with a set of temptations others don't, like vanity, pride, and manipulating people. Those who don't have beauty deal with a different set of temptations, perhaps including jealousy and resentment. The point is God gives different people different gifts by which they serve others. All people are sinners who misuse the gifts God gives them, so the Lord died and rose again for us all.

My advice? Go easy on your sister and go easy on yourself. Rather than covet who you're not, confess your sins and give thanks to God for who you are. You may not realize it for a while, but you'll come to appreciate the Lord's plan down the road a ways.

Why is my brother so much more popular? Why is my sister so much smarter? Why is my brother so much stronger? Why did my sister get all the talent?

These are all variations on the previous question. Whether or not you like the answer, it still applies. Different people have different gifts to serve in different ways. Sinners tend to wish they possessed different gifts from the ones they have. With different gifts, different sinners will face different temptations. Now, you can fix a lot of this: if you want to be stronger—work out. If you want to be smarter—study more. Whatever you do, do your best. But understand the Lord might have different plans from yours, and He knows best (Jeremiah 29:11).

100

My mom married a man with two kids, so now my brother and i have a stepbrother and a stepsister. We're about the same age, but it feels weird. Are we going to be close?

Stepchildren always, always grow to be the best of friends in no time . . . on television; and there, they manage to do it in only a half-hour with commercial breaks! You, however, live in the real world. In the real world, brothers and sisters are close to each other because they've lived under the same roof all their lives. When step-kids get combined into a blended family, y'all haven't been living under the same roof all your lives, so you haven't had the time it takes to build that bond. Furthermore, if you're in high school, you're naturally growing more independent and self-sufficient, which means you're not at a stage where you want to spend a lot of time with the rest of the family. If they're the same age, your step-siblings feel the same way.

So are you going to be close? You might be, but more because you're friends with common interests than because you're family. You might not be, simply because there isn't a lot of time for getting to know each other. Furthermore, there could easily be a fair amount of distrust and tension in the house.

My advice? As you honor your parents (mom and step-dad in this case) treat your siblings with kindness and do your best to be a servant. Where you're a jerk, apologize and ask for forgiveness. At worst, you'll have a civil relationship. You could get to be good friends. You could even develop a relationship closer to that of a real brother or sister.

101

My younger brother wants to hang around with me, but he's so immature. What can i do?

A couple years make a big difference when you're

young. A two-year-old and a five-year-old are worlds apart. A ten-year-old boy and a thirteen-year-old girl will seem like they're from different planets. Hostile planets, even.

As a little brother, I can tell you it seemed like my older sister had all the cool friends; and since she was older, she knew how to do more cool stuff and also had more freedom to do cool things. Thus, I did my best to hang around my big sister when I could . . . though I'm not always sure she appreciated my presence.

That's one of the reasons why a younger sibling will hang around you. Kids want to be like grown-ups. So while you're busy trying to act like a mature college student while you're still in high school, your younger brother is trying to act like you.

102 Of course, another reason could well be less constructive. Younger kids sometimes like to pass the time by bothering other people for no good reason. Your little brother might be bored and looking for someone to annoy. Not that I ever did anything like this, of course. Just ask my sister. No, don't.

What can you do? For one thing, keep in mind you are a role model for your younger siblings. If you can, find some good activities they can do with you. This may seem a bother now, but it will pay off later when you're grown up and your memories of childhood aren't how you were always at each other's throats. More important, though, bring your parents into this discussion. They may have some expectations for you and your siblings you're not aware of.

My sister is always borrowing my clothes, and sometimes she ruins them. Help!

When you're little kids, things like privacy and boundaries don't have a whole lot of meaning; but when you're a teenager, they mean a lot. So while you were younger, you and your sister probably traded lots of stuff back and forth without worrying about permission. It was okay with you then, but it's not anymore. I'd suggest you first try talking to your sister. Explain that you're willing to loan some things, as long as she asks first and returns them in good condition. See if the two of you can just set up some straightforward rules for handling the matter. Handle it nicely instead of screaming when you find your favorite top on the floor in the corner.

Will that work? Maybe, maybe not. If it doesn't, it's time to call in your parents. When they tell you they'd like you to work it out, you can honestly say, "We've already tried, and now we could use your wisdom and fair-mindedness."

103

i don't want to go to my sister's stupid dance recital. What do i do?

Somehow, this sounds like a brother asking the question; and I can understand there are things you'd rather do. Like clean the gravel out of your parents' car tires, or eat grass clippings. On the other hand, the recital is really important to your sister. You can do a lot to strengthen peace in the house by going.

Cheerfully. If you make a big deal about how nice you're trying to be or just grouse your way through it, then everyone knows you're trying to make yourself the annoying martyr and you already have your reward.

My younger siblings get away with a lot more because my parents were a whole lot stricter with me. is that fair?

Probably not, but it's perfectly understandable, especially if you're the firstborn. If you were, keep this in mind, your parents didn't really know how to be parents when you were born. They had to learn by raising you. This means they were probably extra cautious with you: where they'd freak out if you put a dusty finger in your mouth, they might watch complacently while your toddler brother eats mud. Since you're the first, they were probably more strict. This pattern continues. Since you're the oldest, you're also the first teenager they've ever had.

On the other hand, being the firstborn has its share of advantages. Since you were the only child around for a while, you probably got more personal attention when you were small. You likely have greater freedoms now than your younger siblings.

Oh, and one more thing. There's nothing wrong with having strict parents. It's a scary world out there, and you've gotten some good training in self-discipline that's going to pay off.

104

My parents let my brother do something, but now they won't let me. is that fair?

Again, probably not, but that may not be the issue at all.

For instance, let's say your parents let your brother go on a float trip down the river, but they didn't let you. Why? Because you can't swim. I could see parents doing that. Shoot, I'd do that.

Or maybe your brother talked your parents into letting him go to a party, and it ended up with broken furniture and your brother calling your dad from a police officer's cell phone. Again, I could see your parents turning down your request. You're going to tell me you're not your brother, and I know that. So do your parents. I'd simply advise you to respectfully ask for their reasons, honor them, and wait for the trust level to build.

105

My parents have always treated us differently, and it seems to me like they're playing favorites. When they punish me, i have to do something i hate; but when they punish my brother, it doesn't seem so bad. What do you think?

I think that, since you're different, your parents will treat you differently. I have two small boys who react to discipline differently. One of them hates the time-out chair—sitting still for five minutes is the worst punishment imaginable. The other, though, is happy to sit in the corner for a long stretch. He'll examine the texture of the wall and make up a song about it, so it doesn't feel like punishment to him. It doesn't mean that I love one son more than the other: since they're different, I'll treat them differently. Likewise, your parents will treat different children differently. It doesn't mean they're playing favorites.

i found my brother's stash of drugs. What do i do?

Tell your parents. I know, I know! You think you should talk to your brother first. But your brother needs some serious help before he ruins his life. That's your parents' station and responsibility, not yours. Drug users are not known for honesty and cooperation. If you talk to your brother first, he'll likely just move the stash and hide the evidence. That's not going to help him.

i'm an only child. is this good or bad?

You're you, and the Lord in His wisdom chose to make you the sole child of your parents. There are some drawbacks to this—having siblings means you have friends right at home. That's good for learning social skills. On the other hand, you also receive more attention from your parents than kids in large families, and that can help you excel in studies, sports, music, and other areas. It's not particularly good or bad. It simply is the case.

You mentioned Mary and Martha in Luke 10:38—42. i don't get this story. How come Jesus lets Mary sit around while Martha does all the work?

It doesn't seem right, does it? Mary should be serving as much as Martha is. That's what service and station are about. But here's the difference, the Solution is in the room. Jesus is present, sitting in their house and teaching. He's speaking His holy, life-giving Word. By Mary's action of sitting and listening, she's saying, "The Savior is here to forgive me! Compared to that, my work is meaningless." Likewise, Martha's labors indicate that she finds her works more important than listening to the Savior while He's present.

This text isn't really about how sisters get along. After Jesus leaves, Mary had better get back to doing the dishes. It's about Jesus' presence to save, and it teaches us about worship. When we gather in Jesus' name, He's present with us (Matthew 18:20) by His Word and Sacraments. So when we gather for divine service, we're not there to do the Martha thing and show Jesus how hard we're working. We gather to hear His saving Word and receive His body and blood in Holy Communion. His presence with salvation is far more important than our works and labors.

Section Five:
Friends

Friendship can mean a lot of things, from casual running buddies to best friends who remain so for decades. Like brother and sister, this is a tough station to define. All of these relationships have a few things in common, some more and some less. We've got to start somewhere, so let's start with six-year-olds.

As part of my present duties, I'm serving as a school administrator for a little Lutheran elementary school in Idaho. I've made this important discovery:

when you're in first grade, it's easy to find a friend. You meet someone on the playground who also wants to play. If two swings are open, you both swing. If one swing is open, you take turns. If it works well, you agree to meet at the next recess and do it again. If one of you wants to hog the swing all the time, you get in a fight and find another friend. By next recess, all is likely forgiven and forgotten. The more time you spend together, the better friends you get to be.

Sometimes I envy first graders. Life is good when friends come easy. If we use some common sense, we can learn a lot about friendship from some six-year-olds on the playground.

Friendship is often built on common interests, like two little kids who like to swing. If you hate sci-fi and somebody else has actually taken the time to learn how to speak Klingon (vaD quv vo' 'oH, if you know what I mean), you might not have a lot in common. You may in fact be highly annoyed by someone who speaks in inter-galactic languages of war. On the other hand, if you both play basketball, then you've got something to do.

Along with common interests go common values and beliefs. If someone believes illegal street-racing is a fun hobby, while you value, say, being alive, you're proba-bly not going to get along real well. If someone spends all their time attacking Christianity, it's not going to sit well with you very long.

Friendship is also built on serving one another. I'll bet you saw that coming by now! First-graders stay friends when they share the swing. The more friends take care of each other, the stronger the friendship will be. If you want to destroy a friendship, try using pride. No one likes to hang around with somebody who believes he's always better, always right. If you don't like pride, try selfishness, because your friends will fade away if you insist that you should always go first and get your way. Pride and selfishness mean you're hogging the swing. You swing hog, you!

Forgiveness is a big part of friendship. Everyone hogs the swing at times, says the wrong thing, holds the ruler of the Klingon Empire in low esteem, or just acts like a jerk. That's why, whether you're six years old or far older, forgiveness removes the offense so you can get back to being friends.

Time is another big ingredient. Being a servant to somebody else requires time. If you don't spend time cultivating friendships, they won't grow.

110

Along with time, trust is important, too. Trust has to be earned. If you keep promising to show up at the swings and you never make it, you're going to lose friends. Honesty goes a long way to building trust, as does a lot of time of serving. The higher the trust level, the stronger the friendship.

So there you go; ingredients for strong friendship include common interests, mutual service, humility, forgiveness, trust, and time. If all of this is true, then we'd better add a couple more thoughts, which become more apparent, sometimes painfully, as you get older.

You're not going to be friends with everybody. In part this means you simply don't have time to invest in friendship. It also means, because of your interests and values, some people just won't like you. You won't care much for them, either. See chapter 7 about enemies.

Your friends will change. It's bound to happen because of all the variables. In other words, you're not the only one who has to have time, trust, a willingness to serve, common interests, etc. Until you're through the college years, you're pretty much in a transition stage where things are always changing—for you and everybody else your age. Friends move away and new ones show up. You'll lose contact with some and spend more time with others. Is that good or bad? It can be either. It's just the way it is. It's tough to keep even one good friend all the way from ninth grade into your adult years.

Friendship is important, but it's not the only thing. You've got to balance friends with everything else in life. In high school, you might have a heavy class load, **111** tons of homework, sports, clubs, student government, an after-school job and more. All of these can be valuable, and all of them take time. The more time you spend on these, the less time you have to spend with friends, and the friends you're close to will likely be the ones on the same team or in the same class so you're spending time with each other. Life is a gigantic balancing act. If you spend all of your time working, you'll have few friends. If you spend all your time with friends, your grades and employment prospects are going to be low. Your parents aren't going to be real thrilled, either.

In the Bible, the book of Proverbs speaks a lot of divinely inspired common sense about friendships. A common theme is this: pick your friends carefully. We've already noted common interests make for good friendships, but you must be aware that some common interests are downright sinful. Proverbs 22:14–15 warns, "Make no friendship with a man given to anger, nor go with a wrathful man, lest you learn his ways and entangle yourself in a snare." It's easy to pick up the sins and bad attitudes of friends. Likewise, Proverbs 12:26 warns, "The righteous should choose his friends carefully, for the way of the wicked leads them astray" (Proverbs 12:26 NKJV). Ideally, your friends should help you remain faithful to the Lord, not keep trying to pull you away.

Remember, first and foremost, your relationships are governed by God's Law. What He says, goes. Thus the Lord warns in Deuteronomy 13:6 your friend "who is as your own soul" may entice you to worship false gods. Sadly, a lot of Christians are led from the faith because they value their friends' company more than the Lord's love, or just want to fit in with "what everybody else is doing."

Beware of false friendships. Proverbs 19:6 observes, "Many seek the favor of a generous man, and everyone is a friend to a man who gives gifts." A lot of people try to attract friends by spending money, giving gifts, and being popular. I remember a kid in college who was sort of a misfit. He had a lot of friends as long as he bought the alcohol. But as soon as the money was gone, the friends disappeared as well. Why? Because, they weren't friends! They were leeches who just want a good time, and were willing to fake friendship for a free drink.

True friends stick together when others leave. Proverbs 17:17 says, "A friend loves at all times, and a brother is born for adversity." Furthermore, a friend is willing to disagree and point out when you're being a jerk, a move that requires both courage and love. A friend's criticism is a lot more helpful than a foe's flattery; or as Proverbs 27:6 puts it, "Faithful are the wounds of a friend; profuse are the kisses of an enemy." We all need friends who love us enough to call us to repentance.

For whatever reasons, you'll make and lose friends, often due to circumstances beyond your control. That's life in a sinful, uncertain, ever-changing world. What doesn't change, though, is Jesus' love for you. In John 15:13, Jesus tells His disciples, "Greater love has no one than this, that someone lays down his life for his friends." That's true. The ultimate act of service is to die for another. But Jesus isn't talking about just anyone. In the next verse, He calls the disciples His friends, and **113** He's on His way to the cross to lay down His life for them.

The Lord Jesus has gone to that cross for you, too, giving His life to win forgiveness and salvation for you. You were once an enemy of God, but Jesus calls you His friend, and Proverbs 18:24 is never more true than when it says of Jesus: "A man of many companions may come to ruin, but there is a friend who sticks closer than a brother." Indeed, Jesus still "sticks close," speaking His Word to you and giving you His body and blood in Holy Communion. Even if you're at a time when you have no friends, you're not alone. The Lord is with you.

Q&A:
You Ask . . .

What does vaD quv vo' 'oH mean, anyway?

"For the honor of it." At least, if the Klingon translation Web site was telling the truth. The Internet is always right, isn't it . . . ?

if an author of a book believes the internet is always right, should i rely on his advice?

Not if he's serious, no. He's probably one of those

guys with a fixation for Klingons.

i've been sitting in biology class next to this guy for a couple of weeks, so i guess we're sort of friends. He just asked me if he could borrow $20. i said, "No." He said, "Don't you trust me?" Should i loan him the money?

I wouldn't. Trust has to be earned, and that takes time. When a newcomer asks me to trust them, they either (a) don't understand trust or (b) want to guilt-trip me into helping them because I feel bad about not trusting them. Keep your money. If he continues, ask for a different seat.

115

My friend and i have been friends for a long time. Suddenly, it seems like the friendship is falling apart. What's happening?

There's a bunch of possibilities, so you may want to sit back and take a long inventory.

Are there new people in the mix?
Do you or your friend have a new friend? Maybe a crush on someone? When you spend more time with one, you have less time for others. If your

friend has found somebody new, I'd recommend rolling with it for a while and seeing if things settle down. If you've got a new friend, then you need to figure out how you want to balance your time; I'd recommend keeping your old friend, too. Good friends are hard to find.

Are there new responsibilities in the mix? An after-school job or joining a sports team is going to take up a lot of time. In that case, you may have to make some extra effort to see each other and stay friends.

Has something big happened? Maybe your friend's parents are having marriage problems, and your friend is depressed and confused. In that case, it's good to make it known you're available just to be around. If you're the one in a troubled family, you might just tell your friend, "Things are tough right now. I may not be the best friend at the moment. Please be patient with me."

Is there a big life change ahead? If you're both a month from graduation and four months from college, then you may be looking to what lies ahead. That may have both of you forgetting what's happening now, or getting ready to go your separate ways.

116

Did you have a big fight? Fights don't necessarily destroy friendships, but continued misunderstandings do. You might have had an argument where you were both wrong, but neither is willing to admit it. Or you might be in a situation where you just have to suck it up and overlook your friend's fault to keep the friendship going.

Or . . . it may just be the two of you are growing apart as you mature and find new interests and goals. As I mentioned earlier, you're in a time when everything's changing quickly, and a lot of friendships fade. A lot of new ones form, too. It's the nature of your age.

117

Bottom line: friendships are built on service, time, and work. As long as the two of you are willing and able to work at your friendship, it will remain. In the real world, the two of you may not always be both willing and able.

What are "friends with benefits"?

They're sinners who need to read chapter 8 about sex. Since this isn't really about friendship. We'll talk about it there.

Can i have non-Christian friends?

Yes. Unless you live in a Christian commune on a small island, this is likely going to happen. The Bible says in order to not associate with unbelievers, "you would need to go out of the world" (1 Corinthians 5:10). On the other hand, it also warns, "Therefore whoever wishes to be a friend of the world makes himself an enemy of God" (James 4:4).

You need to be responsible and understand where the two of you are different. As a Christian, you operate by God's Law. There's a right and a wrong, and you're striving to do the right thing because the wrong thing is sin, which has consequences. For a non-Christian living in the world, it's very likely he believes right and wrong aren't so clear-cut, things are "right" as long as you enjoy them and no one gets hurt. As a Christian, and as a good friend, you need to make sure you decide right and wrong activities in your friendship based on God's Word, not your friend's opinions.

Furthermore, a non-Christian isn't going to comprehend the importance of the Gospel. Your friend may poke fun or even try to talk you out of the faith—not out of malice, but simply because he's true to his own beliefs. There's always a temptation to adopt a friend's opinions because you don't want to harm the friendship. But your friend hasn't died to redeem you, nor can he raise you from the dead. Jesus has died for both of you, and He can raise the both of you. Make sure your friendships don't pull you away from Christ, or else you and your friends will be lost.

My friend wants me to cover for him while he's _____. if his mom calls and asks me if he's at my house, i'm supposed to say he just left. Should i do it? After all, we're good friends.

It doesn't matter what sin you fill in the blank with, the world has this expectation that you'll cover for your friends to keep them out of trouble. It happens a lot. It doesn't make this a good thing. In any case, you have a friend who's asking you to lie and deceive his mom so he can disobey her. When you ask a friend to cover for you, you're doing the same thing.

Sorry, but friends don't ask friends to lie for them. That's not serving one another according to God's Word, rather enticing a friend into sin. Tell your friend you won't cover for him. If he gets mad that you're doing the right thing, that's his problem—not yours. If he doesn't want to be your friend because you did the right thing, then it's his loss—not yours.

Furthermore, if you cover for him, you're helping him keep his bad habit and partaking of his sin.

My friend wants me to help her cheat on the math exam. She has to pass this class to stay on track for graduation! Should i help her?

See the previous question. Friends don't ask friends to cheat. You are asking them to violate their faith and sin. You can help your friend by not helping and telling her why, instead of helping her continue a pattern of cheating that's going to hurt her in the future.

Furthermore, chances are you're not going to be friends for the rest of your life, but you still have to live with you. Even for just this life, you'd be wise to preserve your own integrity over helping someone sin. In the long run, you'll have a clean conscience and a reputation that enables you to help more people with honest needs. You'll also be in the habit of being honest, and it's a lot easier to be honest when you've made it your practice.

120

A bunch of my high school friends are going to a drinking party Friday night. i don't drink, so they asked me if i'd drive for them. Should i be the safety patrol?

Let me get this straight. First, your friends are going to an underage drinking party, which means it's illegal. So you're asking me for permission to be an accessory. Second, high school drinking parties usually don't involve somber individuals holding wine glasses with their pinkies sticking out while discussing geopolitics. They get out of hand pretty quickly, and normally involve vandalism, stupidity, and copious amounts of vomit.

For those who stay sober, it's a horrible thing to watch. And smell! It also means a bunch of your peers are going to keep offering you drinks, perhaps making fun of you when you say no. The pressure to give in can be intense. If you do, you're still the one with the keys to the car. Except now you can't see straight, but you'll still feel the need to drive your friends home. If you get pulled over now, they're not the ones in *big* trouble.

I don't see how this is a good idea. Tell your friends you're busy doing something smarter, like counting coats of varnish on various pieces of woodwork around your house. Even better, tell them to ask their parents for a ride. What? They can't do that for obvious reasons? Then why are they asking you? For obvious reasons. Stay sober. Stay safe. Stay home.

Looking back, I've answered three questions in a row about friends who want you to do something wrong. Reminder: after high school graduation, most of these people won't be your friends for much longer, even the one who seem like really good friends now. You've got approximately sixty years of life left after high school. Friends are important, but these present relationships are mostly temporary. Don't risk or mess up your life, your health, or your reputation when you've got so much future left to go.

i'm lonely.
Why don't i have many friends?

Sometimes, this is just situational, like when you

121

move to a new school and don't know anybody. This can just take care of itself.

It may be a matter of personal hygiene. Seriously! You may want to give yourself a once-over and make sure you're presentable. You don't have to be stunning, but it helps if you don't smell bad or have breakfast left on your face.

Every now and then, it's because you've been targeted. Kids have been known to bully by getting others to shun you. (For more, see chapter 7 on enemies.)

It may also be a matter of personality. People who are outgoing tend to have a lot of friends. People who are more reserved tend to have fewer friends. Both have advantages. People with a lot of friends have less time for each one, while people with few friends have more time and thus may have deeper relationships. Furthermore, it's often the introverts who get the better grades in school, since they're not distracted by a bunch of people all the time. If you're planning on college, keep in mind universities award scholarships for brains and skill, not popularity.

All the same, it stinks to be lonely. My advice? Pray about it. The Lord has promised He won't forsake you, and He'll provide you with all that you need—in His time, according to His will. In the meantime, beware of an idle mind. Use the time alone constructively to read, exercise, learn a new hobby. Sitting down and giving in to loneliness stands a good chance of leading you into depression, and that's not going to help. Learning and doing more will keep you occupied . . . and may lead to some new friends.

Always remember God made you to be you for His reasons. He's made you His own in Baptism. You are not alone.

i just went out on a date with my best friend's ex-boyfriend, and now she won't talk to me. What did i do wrong?

Let's think this through. When a couple breaks up after even a small length of time, it's not an emotionally clean break. There's anger or sorrow; maybe there's relief if the guy was a jerk.

In this case, you went out with your best friend's ex-boyfriend because (a) your best friend wasn't seeing him anymore, and (b) you were attracted to him. If your best friend is angry about the breakup because she didn't want to break up with him, she's going to see you as taking his side—and making sure they can't get back together. I'm not saying they would, but she might see it that way. If she's sad, she could use a friend right now . . . but her best friend is dating the guy who broke her heart. If she broke up with him because he's a jerk, then she probably doesn't want to see you get hurt like she did. *So, any idea why she isn't talking to you right now?*

"She needs to get over it," you might be thinking. While this may be true, maybe you could use some sensitivity training instead of selfishly grabbing the ex. I don't know the situation enough to make a clear judgment, so I'll leave it to you to examine yourself. In the meantime, no matter who's at fault here, this *is* true: if you keep the boyfriend, you'll lose the best friend. It may work out for your happiness: he may be the guy you marry and spend the rest of your life with. He may dump you next week. But if you keep him, you lose her. That's just how it is. Actions have consequences.

My friend said she's thinking about suicide, but made me promise not to tell anyone. What do i do?

Tell someone, like her parents or a trusted teacher. If she's thinking about ending her life, she needs some professional help from people who have the right training. Will you break the promise you made? Yes. Would you rather have a friend who's alive and maybe mad at you for a while, or attend her funeral? This isn't about friendship—it's about preserving life God has given.

124

A good friend is a great gift from God. The rules are pretty clear: the more work you put into a relationship, the more you get out of it. That's life. And—this is one of the few times you'll hear me say this in this book— that's fair. I like having friends. The work is worth doing.

Even better is the promise from Proverbs 18:24, we have a friend who sticks closer than a brother. Jesus' relationship with you is not one of equal effort. Long before you were born, He did everything to make you His forever. While friendships come and go, His promise remains true in Word and Sacrament: "And behold, I am with you always, to the end of the age" (Matthew 28:20).

Section Six: Coworkers, Teammates, Students, and Others

There are people you hang around with a lot. You have common interests and goals. You might even trust them. It's just you wouldn't exactly call them friends.

They're coworkers, teammates, fellow students,

and others. For want of a better term, you share the station of "servant" under a common master. The reason you hang around them is you have to. It's part of the job, or the team, or the classroom. The reason you have common goals is because, well, you have to. If it's at work, you all have the common goal of making money. If it's a team, the goal is winning. If it's a classroom, it's experiencing the joy of instruction and drinking deeply from the fountain of knowledge, rejoicing in the sheer pleasure of intellectual stimulation. Or else it's Algebra 2, in which case you just want to pass the class and keep going. I sure hope my wife, the math teacher, doesn't read this.

Now, you'll get along with some of these people, and some might even be friends. Chances are, though, some of them will be not-so-easy to get along with. There will **127** be those who seem to enjoy (a) nacho-cheese breath and (b) belching in your general direction. There will be those who can't stop talking at work long enough, say, to actually do any work. There will be those who are more than happy to let you do all the research for the class project and take the credit for your labor. And there will be those with dirty minds and mouths who can't stop polluting the air around them with jokes, observations, and words that I shan't mention here.

So whether you like your coworkers or not, how should you treat them? For this little section, we're going to operate with the following basic understandings. You won't find a lot of Scripture verses below, because we've already covered them in previous sections.

a. In any group or on any team you are a part of, you can be sure every member is sinful. This means everyone in the group is going to bring in their share of selfishness, hang-ups, annoyances, and problems.

b. The world is full of obnoxious people. The chances of your group not having obnoxious persons is pretty remote.

c. You can't control other people. You can only control you. And sometimes, you can be pretty obnoxious, too.

d. You don't necessarily have to like coworkers, but you do need to work with them.

128 e. Working toward a goal involves some tasks that aren't enjoyable. Working on a team usually involves an authority figure, like a boss, a coach, or a teacher. These two facets give your old sinful nature lots to complain about. You will find that many others' old sinful natures feel the same way.

f. Yes, the Fourth Commandment applies to the boss, coach, and teacher.

g. As a Christian within this group, you have the privilege of being a servant to others. This means you are also helping them work toward the group's goal and their personal success, even as you properly honor the one who's in charge of the group.

h. As a Christian, you also have the privilege of being an example, "In the same way, let your light shine before others, so that they may see your good works and give glory to your Father who is in heaven" (Matthew 5:16). You don't leave your Christianity in the locker when you arrive; your faith should influence all you do.

i. At times, you may find yourself in the awkward situation of being caught between your equals and the boss. If you remain loyal to your peers, it's good for team unity, but you may end up dishonoring the authority. If you honor the authority, you may destroy team unity and what the authority is trying to accomplish. In this sinful world, there may not be an easy solution. Remember, you are to honor God before any human authorities or peers.

j. In your high school and college years, everything is in flux, the goals aren't permanent. Bad situations are usually temporary. In other words, a terrible job may only last the summer until school starts, it's not like you're climbing down into the mine shaft for the next forty years. The team is only going to be together for three months until the season ends. If you're in a crummy situation, you can take heart that it's likely not going to last very long. Grit your teeth and bear it. Better times are coming.

129

But whether the current times and jobs are good or bad, the Lord hasn't changed. Indeed:

> Have this mind among yourselves,
> which is yours in Christ Jesus, who,
> though He was in the form of God,

did not count equality with God a thing to be grasped, but made Himself nothing, taking the form of a servant, being born in the likeness of men. And being found in human form, He humbled Himself by becoming obedient to the point of death, even death on a cross. **(Philippians 2:5–8)**

Your worth doesn't depend on the assignment, the team record or the job; nor does it depend on how well you get along with your coworkers. Your worth is built upon Jesus Christ, who took on the form of a servant to do the worst job of all—suffering cross and hell to save you from sin. His loyalty and faithfulness won't change, because He's died to make you His forever. Oh, yes—better times are coming.

130

Q&A:
You Ask . . .

i close down the store with one other employee. He's more than happy to sit around and play on the computer while i do all the work. What should i do?

Don't buy an electronic cattle prod, as tempting as the idea might be. Think this through according to station. Your coworker's sin is one of sloth. That's why he's failing to serve as he should. So, whose job is it to make sure he works? If the boss has made you the shift supervisor, then you've got the station. If not, then this isn't your fight. You can ask him for help, maybe even give specific ideas of what he could be doing. It might help. It might not.

Either way, just keep doing your job. The more you do, the better you'll be at your work. Bosses aren't dumb. They want good employees who do the work, and they'll be checking around to see how things are going. You'll get rewarded for doing the work, while the other guy won't. Unless, of course, you've got one of those bosses who's just unfair.

i've got a boss who's just unfair. i just know he has it out for me. What do i do?

132

First off, be completely honest with yourself. Have you done anything that would make your boss not like you or trust you? If you brought this upon yourself, then it's up to you to work to rebuild the trust. Sure, you can quit and find another job, but your new boss will call your old one for a recommendation . . . or wonder why you didn't tell where you previously worked on your job application.

However, some bosses just aren't fair. At my first job, a new boss took over a few months after I got there. I couldn't help but notice, within six months, I was the only guy still on the staff. I also noticed, as time went on, newer employees kept getting promoted past me; 'twas a bit annoying telling my new supervisors what they should be telling me to do. I'm not sure what I did, but that boss didn't like me. After 18 months of work, though, he did give me a raise: from $3.10 to $3.15! A nickel!

So what did I do? I kept working there through the end of summer, doing my best to do the job and honor my boss. Then I quit in order to focus on my senior year of high school. Then I got a different job. This is the nice thing about part-time jobs in high school—you can usually find another one. Until you do, though, I'd advise you to honor your unfair boss and do your job.

My friend just invited me to apply for a job where he works. The pay is great, but the job description says, "Must be able to tolerate strong sewage odors." What do you think?

I'm thankful that, if you take that job with the great pay, you won't need to come to my house for dinner at the end of the shift. Besides, this isn't a question about coworkers. Focus, please.

i got assigned to a class project where the other students are all happy to let me do all the work. They know i care about the grade more than they do. What can i do?

This is pretty similar to the question about the

133

employee who wants to let you do all the work, but let's answer it anyway—in a different way. You're going to encounter a lot of people in life who want a free ride at your expense, and this is just another example.

So think it through. What are your choices? You should ask them to pitch in and share the work fairly, but it doesn't mean they're going to. Instead, they'll probably spend the next five minutes flattering you to try to get you to feel good about doing all the work they have no intention of doing. You can yell at them, but we've already established they don't care that much. You can complain to the teacher, who is probably going to give you the "this is a good chance to learn how to interact with other people" speech. You can just not do the work, in which case everyone will fail—which will hurt you more than others because we already established they don't care that much.

So, here's my two cents. Honor your teacher and fulfill your station of student by doing the work. If your fellow students don't want to help, it's their loss. Sure, they may get the same grade you do—or not, if your teacher is observing all this—but they're only training themselves to use other people and stay dumb. You, on the other hand, have learned something and kept your commitment to your station intact.

Okay, but aren't i enabling them to be lazy and use the work of others for personal gain?

you ask about . . . RELATIONSHIPS

Okay, I'll spot you that one, but unless you've got a better idea I think my answer is still the best. Your teacher has the station of threatening them to shape up or else. I'm just telling you to stay true to your own work ethic.

i believe in working hard while i'm on the job, staying busy and putting in a day's work for a day's pay. My fellow workers are accusing me of trying to suck up to the boss. What do i do?

This question may not be as easy to answer as it sounds. On the one hand, your coworkers may just be lazy. In that case, I wouldn't care too much if they criticized me for working hard.

On the other hand, in some job situations, employees have worked out deals with the management so they need a certain number of people to do a certain amount of work. If you start working hard and accomplishing more than the agreement calls for, then you're demonstrating that (a) the company should ask the employees to do more work, or (b) the company doesn't need as many employees to get the usual work done. Your fellow employees won't appreciate either one, which may be why they want you to slow down.

If that's the case, believe it or not, your boss might want you to slow down a little, too. The company's going to get a lot more done if everybody's getting along than not. If you keep pushing ahead, you could

135

end up as a sore spot between employees and the management. Isn't that special?

So what do you do? Here's a thought. Slow down—at least a little, and do whatever you do as well as you can do it. Give it a few days, then ask the boss for a quick performance evaluation. Don't say, "The guys told me to slow down, so I did." Try, "Since I'm still pretty new around here, I just wanted to make sure that I was doing okay." If he's happy with what you're doing and your coworkers are okay with you, that's probably the best you can do. Is it sin-free? I honestly don't know, but it's the best you can do in a sinful world with sinful people. Thanks be to God you're not saved by your job performance, but by Jesus' work and cross.

This girl i work with wants to spend the whole shift telling me about her personal problems. it's driving me crazy, and i can't get my work done. Any suggestions?

This is one of those times where you need to balance the need of the individual and the tasks you're given to do. You've got your station of employee and your tasks to do, but it's also going to help if you can be a sympathetic ear. Maybe this will work: "It sounds like you need to talk, so maybe we could chat for fifteen minutes at break before getting back to work." Or if you want to skip this step, "I understand you have a few things going on, and I'll keep you in my prayers. Right now, you'll have to excuse me because I need to get this work done." Beyond that, you're pretty much stuck. Once again, it's the boss who has the station of telling an employee to get to work. It's not going to go well if you take over the boss's job.

My fellow workers are obnoxious. They're crude and always throw the F-word around, and they make everything into a dirty joke. What can i do?

I'm with you. I hate it when people start talking about funiculars. That's what you meant, right?

What to do? You can't change them, so make sure you know that up front. You can ask them to watch the language, and they might; but if they like talking that way, you're not going to get them to clean up their act. All you can do is do your job, keep your standards, and try to your best to get along anyway. Maybe it'll set an example for them.

Bear in mind some jobs allow for obnoxious behavior more than others. A work environment away from the public (construction, road repair, etc.) usually allows for a lot more crude humor. Jobs that involve interacting with the public and customers generally require better manners. You might want to keep this in mind when you're looking at different jobs.

137

Every time i ride the bus to soccer practice, one of the midfielders always tells a dirty joke. He's made it his goal to make me laugh at one by the end of the season, and he says i'll fit in better if i do. Advice?

My advice is that you stay true to your high standards and don't join in the laugh; if you do, you'll reward him for his efforts to drag you down. There are worse things in life than suffering ridicule from foulmouthed idiots.

That's pretty much what he is. The team's not going to accept you because you laugh at dirty jokes. The team is going to accept you if you play hard, work well with others, and contribute to the effort. If the team is all about crude humor instead of soccer, then you probably want to find a different team.

My teammates want me to join in on a practical joke. What do you think?

Practical jokes are, um, funny things. That is, they can be funny or not. They can be harmless gags that bring a team together or destructive acts that break it apart. Some things to consider: Is the joke itself harmless or destructive? Harmless is okay; avoid destructive. Do players want to do it out of fun, or because they want to pick on somebody? The first can be humorous; the second is bullying. Is the intended vic-

138

tim a good sport, or is it going to hurt them? Some people can take a good joke. Some can't. A good practical joke can build team unity, victim included. A bad one just isn't funny at all.

You said that i shouldn't leave my Christianity in the locker when i go on the job, so how much should i be witnessing to my coworkers?

When you're working, your station requires you to serve your employer by doing your job. If you spend your time evangelizing fellow cooks when you're supposed to be preparing meals, you're not doing what you were hired to do. If the customer comes in for an oil change and you recite the Catechism to them, you're not doing what you were hired to do.

139

Now, I've run into Christians who believe in this sort of in-your-face witnessing, as if you're not evangelizing if everybody in earshot isn't annoyed with you for talking about Jesus. If they end up getting fired for not doing their job, they may even proclaim they're being persecuted.

Here's a text to keep in mind:

> In your hearts regard Christ the Lord
> as holy, always being prepared to
> make a defense to anyone who asks
> you for a reason for the hope that is in
> you; yet do it with gentleness and
> respect, having a good conscience, so

that, when you are slandered, those
who revile your good behavior in
Christ may be put to shame.
(1 Peter 3:15–16)

Be "prepared" when someone "asks you." In other
words, go about your work with the dedication of one
who seeks to serve in the station you have. As you get
to know people, conversations will start. Unless you're
trying to hide it, they're going to find out that you're a
Christian. As they grow to trust you, they may start
asking questions. There you are, evangelizing because
they want you to. That's the sort of evangelism you
have the privilege of doing on the job.

I used to work on a parking lot in downtown
Seattle, not exactly a town synonymous with Christian
values and moral purity. As I recall, I was the only
Christian in the bunch of employees—and it was obvious as soon as they asked me what I was studying in
college, and I said I was preparing to be a pastor. As
we got to know each other, we'd get to talking and I'd
have a chance to speak the Gospel. By then, it didn't
annoy them: they were interested in my point of view.
If my point of view happened to be the Word of God,
with the Holy Spirit at work, so much the better! I
don't have any conversion stories from that job to tell
you, but the Lord promises He faithfully cultivates
where His Word is spread, it does not return to Him
empty.

142 Section Seven:
Enemies, Con
Artists, and
Other Annoying
People

Life is full of all sorts of uncertainties, so are relationships. Friends are made and lost. People come and
go. Your plans take all sorts of twists and turns. It's
very unpredictable. There are few guarantees.

But if you're looking for a guarantee when it
comes to relationships, here's one, you're going to

have enemies. Isn't that just super? And you thought the uncertainties were bothersome . . . No matter what stations you hold in life, there will be people who do not like you. There will also be people that you don't like. There will be people who want to cheat you out of money, goods, or reward. There will even be people who actively work to hurt you one way or another. Let's divide these people into a few categories. They might be your enemies because:

1. You are something they are not.

It might be they wanted a certain job or student council position, and you got it instead. It might be you live in a country they don't care for very much. It might be your skin color is different from theirs. It might be you're wealthier or poorer than they are. This is enmity spawned by jealousy, greed, or prejudice.

143

2. You're a mark.

There are lots of people out there who have decided, rather than make an honest living, it's better to con people out of their honest earnings. Con artists are thick upon the land, and they'll target you as their mark. Like they say in the movies, it's nothing personal. It's just business.

3. They're bullies.

Some people just enjoy picking on others because it makes them feel powerful. Rather than live to serve others, they feel good when they're forcing others to obey them. Sad, really.

4. They're crazy, and they just happened to pick you.

Sadly, this happens. Somewhere on the highways and byways of America is a man I met a few years back. In his world—which wasn't particularly the same one we live in, as far as I could tell—his wife supposedly cheated on him with a pastor down around Alabama. He decided he could set things right by hitchhiking around America, picking a pastor at random and beating the stuffing out of him. He chose me. Thanks be to God the beating never took place. I now have an unlisted home number, and I'm a big fan of the Idaho State Patrol. The way his mind works, he's probably forgotten me a long time ago. But it's still a little creepy to know he's out there.

5. You stand for something.

If you stand for anything at all, people are going to stand against you. If you speak up for virtues like sexual purity or respecting authority, people are going to get mad and declare you narrow-minded, intolerant, and worse. It might not be a rational, "I'm upset so let's talk about this" sort of anger. It might be a screaming diatribe, slander on the bathroom wall, or a cruelly orchestrated instant messaging campaign on the internet. If you stand for anything at all, people will oppose you. The more good you try to do, the more heat you're going to catch. That's why the old saying is true, *you will* be known by the friends you have . . . and the enemies you have. It's also why the next category is especially true.

6. You're a Christian.

Jesus Himself makes this very, very clear:

> If the world hates you, know that it has hated Me before it hated you. If you were of the world, the world would love you as its own; but because you are not of the world, but I chose you out of the world, therefore the world hates you. Remember the word that I said to you, "A servant is not greater than his master." If they persecuted Me, they will also perse- cute you. **(John 15:18–20a)**

145

It goes without saying that Jesus had enemies. When He stood before Pilate and Caiaphas, the deci- sion to kill Him wasn't even close. The world hated Him because the world is captive to sin, and "the mind that is set on the flesh is hostile to God, for it does not submit to God's law; indeed, it cannot" (Romans 8:7). When push comes to shove, the world can't help itself—it opposes Jesus. If the world hates Jesus, the world is going to hate you, too. Look out, because it gets worse, the fact you are a Christian could make enemies out of your own family. Jesus says:

> Do not think that I have come to bring peace to the earth. I have not come to bring peace, but a sword. For I have come to set a man against his father, and a daughter against her mother, and a daughter-in-law against her mother-in-law. And a person's enemies will be those of his own household. **(Matthew 10:34–36)**

Out here in Idaho, we have a significant Mormon population. Mormonism, (aka the Church of Jesus Christ of Latter Day Saints, or LDS) is a false religion. Though one must admire the emphasis it puts on strong family values. I know several people who have left the LDS and been baptized in the Christian Church. They rejoice to know and be known by the true Jesus, who died for them, but they also have to endure the sharp pain of family anger and pressure to renounce the grace of God and return to false belief. Having your family push you to forsake Jesus is a horrible cross to bear, but the devil's going to do his best to make you hurt for being a Christian.

7. It's your fault.

Ouch. You did something wrong, and you hurt someone. Don't think you're above this, because you're made of sinful flesh, too. You'll do or say stupid things and hurt people. At this point, they're either your enemy because you've held fast to your sin, refused to confess it and ask them for forgiveness; or else you apologized, but they're embittered and unwilling to forgive. You can fix the first situation— and you need to. You can't do much about the second.

You're going to have enemies, for a bunch of different reasons. Don't fool yourself, this is going to hurt, sometimes very badly. Not only is it going to cause you grief and worry, but you're made of the same sinful flesh as they are. That means you're going to be tempted to act like an enemy and attack back in all sorts of sinful ways. Throughout your life, this is going to be a major pain. So what do you do? Consider the following words of the Lord:

> But I say to you who hear, Love your enemies, do good to those who hate you, bless those who curse you, pray for those who abuse you. To one who strikes you on the cheek, offer the other also, and from one who takes away your cloak do not withhold your tunic either. **(Luke 6:27–29)**

147

We'll throw in one more:

> Repay no one evil for evil, but give thought to do what is honorable in the sight of all. If possible, so far as it depends on you, live peaceably with all. Beloved, never avenge yourselves, but leave it to the wrath of God, for it is written, "Vengeance is mine, I will

repay, says the Lord." To the contrary, "if your enemy is hungry, feed him; if he is thirsty, give him something to drink; for by so doing you will heap burning coals on his head." Do not be overcome by evil, but overcome evil with good. **(Romans 12:17–21)**

There you go: love your enemies. That's all you've got to do. Follow all those commands, and you'll be in good shape.

But before you go out and start loving your enemies, read on a little further. There are two really important points that you need to understand.

First, take a good long look at Luke 6. Who is Jesus talking to, and why is He giving these commands? He's talking to the Pharisees, men who believe you earn your salvation by keeping God's rules and commands. The Pharisees fooled themselves into thinking they could actually keep God's laws well enough to earn heaven. But how well is "well enough" in God's eyes? To earn heaven by your works, you have to keep all of God's rules perfectly—no sinner can do that. You can't get to heaven by keeping God's rules well enough. It's impossible. That's the part that the Pharisees didn't understand. So in Luke 6, Jesus challenges the Pharisees, calling them to repent for their false belief. In other words, He's saying, "So you believe you keep God's laws well enough to earn eternal life? Then let's talk about how well you have to keep God's laws. Let's use how you treat enemies as an example. If you're going to be perfect, then love your enemies. When they hurt you, repay them with kindness. If they slap you across the face, don't slap back. In fact, don't even get mad enough to think that you'd like to slap them back. If you're going to earn God's love by your works, that's how good you have to be."

So why is Jesus telling them this—to give them some pointers on what they can do? Nope. He's telling them what they can't do. His purpose isn't to challenge them to work even harder at earning salvation, but to demonstrate they *can't* earn it. His purpose is to show they fail and sin and fall short of God's favor. His purpose is to show them they need Him to be their Savior, to die on the cross to take away their sins.

That's also you, even though you should love your enemies, you can't love your enemies as you should. **149** Never think you're a Christian because of how you treat your enemies. Never think you're not a Christian because you've failed to love your enemies. You're a Christian because Jesus died for all of your sins, and you believe this because the Holy Spirit has given you faith.

The second point is this, life is extremely messy and complicated, so make sure you know what "love" means and who all you're required to love. In relationships, "love" and "servanthood" go together, right? Therefore, loving your enemies doesn't necessarily mean doing whatever they want. It means doing what is best for them.

Let me give you an example. Occasionally, someone shows up at church for money. They usually have a hard-luck story involving the following elements: they're from out-of-town, just passing through, they belong to a Lutheran Church far away but can't remember the pastor's name, and someone is in need of urgent medical treatment that usually isn't covered by health insurance. Some of these stories are pathetically, obviously false. Some of them are really quite convincing. So, you make the call: being a Christian and a pastor, should I give them money? After all, I'm supposed to love my neighbor and help the poor. Should I help them or not?

I almost always say no. Often, like I said, the story is obviously false and changing as they tell it. They're running a con, lying to get money. If I give it to them, I'm encouraging them to keep lying and conning others. When the stories are more convincing, experience says that I'm dealing with better con artists. Furthermore, whenever I give money to these people, it takes money away—either from my family or from other work of the congregation. In helping a con artist, I'm hurting others.

Now, is it possible I've said no to people who were being honest with me? It is, and I'll never know. Have I helped people who were lying to me? Sure. When you help people, especially strangers, expect nothing in return. At the end of one of these episodes, I confess all my sins—where I helped who I shouldn't have, and didn't help who I should. And I give thanks to God I'm not saved by my ability to sense a con. I'm saved because Jesus forgives me for all of my sins.

I mentioned the guy from the South who wanted to

give me a beating. Since him, I've seriously revised my rules of what I'll do and where I'll go to help people as a pastor. After all, I also have the stations of "husband" and "father," and me dying at the hands of a sociopath isn't going to help me serve my wife and kids much. I'm a mortal, sinful man. Even though I'm commanded to help every neighbor, I can't do it. Neither can you. That's why we give thanks we're not saved by loving neighbors, friends, and enemies. Salvation is ours for the sake of Jesus, who prayed for His enemies even on the cross: "Father, forgive them, for they know not what they do" (Luke 23:34).

You're not a Christian because of how well you treated your enemies today. You're a Christian because Jesus died to turn you from His enemy into His beloved child.

Even so, you're supposed to love your enemies, and you certainly have to deal with them, so let's take some questions.

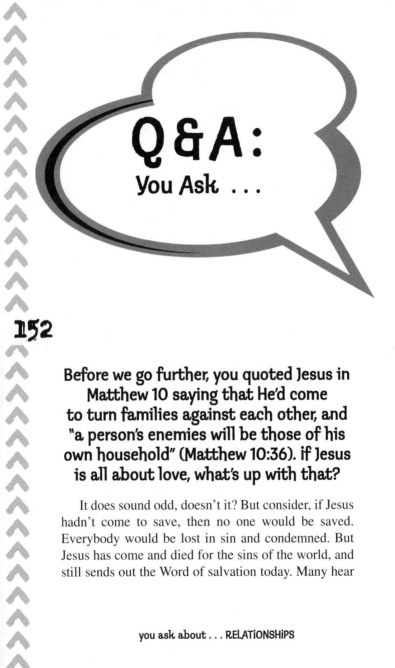

Q & A:
You Ask . . .

Before we go further, you quoted Jesus in
Matthew 10 saying that He'd come
to turn families against each other, and
"a person's enemies will be those of his
own household" (Matthew 10:36). if Jesus
is all about love, what's up with that?

It does sound odd, doesn't it? But consider, if Jesus
hadn't come to save, then no one would be saved.
Everybody would be lost in sin and condemned. But
Jesus has come and died for the sins of the world, and
still sends out the Word of salvation today. Many hear

and believe. Many don't believe. Sometimes, a family is divided down the middle; some believe, and some don't. This can lead to some big family fights, even open hostility.

Before Jesus, then, everyone in the family got along because all were lost in sin. After Jesus, some believe and some don't, leading to problems. Was it better before Jesus? No. The only reason there's strife is not all are lost in sin anymore. That's what Jesus meant when He said He came to turn families against each other: He knew some would believe . . . that's a good thing.

it's been a nightmare! All my friends suddenly stopped talking to me, and i didn't know why. But i just found out another girl at school has been telling lies about me in e-mails and instant messaging. What do i do?

153

This is the latest form of bullying, called cyber-bullying, and seems to be more popular among girls than guys. It's especially cruel because the victim of a normal bully usually knows it as he pulls himself back out of the garbage can. But with cyber-bullying, the whole thing can happen without the victim knowing who, how, or why. Some victims have lapsed into deep depression and self-doubt.

What do you do? Cyber-bullying can be a crime. Talk to your tech teacher or school resource officer, and see what sorts of evidence can be gathered, especially if it was done on school computers. If you want to confront and talk to the cyber-bully, I would recommend you do so with an adult present. If they've gotten this nasty, I wouldn't deal with them one on one. After all, from your description this is a school discipline issue, and it's the principal's station to deal with it, hopefully involving the bully's parents, too.

One other tough thing about cyber-bullying is it usually goes after your reputation. When a bully takes your lunch money, you recover quickly. A good name can be tougher to get back. Hopefully, the truth about the cyber-bully will come out. Until it does, remember your worth isn't based on what is said about you by others, or what others think is true. Your true worth is based on the fact you are a child of God, bought at the price of Jesus' death. Your value isn't going to go away, no matter what an e-mail says.

Somebody hurt me badly. Very badly! No matter how hard i try, i can't forgive them even though i know i should. Am i going to hell?

Christians have sometimes taught Jesus can't forgive you until you forgive others; this might be a bad understanding of the Fifth Petition of the Lord's Prayer—"and forgive us our trespasses, as we forgive those who trespass against us."

Let's run this through some good doctrine. Are you

saved by grace, solely by what Jesus has done for you? Yes! Are you saved by works, by what you do? No! Therefore, to say, "I can't be saved until I forgive my enemy" can't be true, because it says you are saved by your work of forgiving others.

Frankly, if someone hurt you badly enough, you may not be able to forgive them in your lifetime. Pray for them—not their destruction, but that the Lord would be merciful to them as He is to you. Confess your sins, including your inability to forgive. The Lord promises forgiveness for all of your sins—by grace you are saved.

"Joe" doesn't like me at all. Do i have to go near him?

155

That all depends on his station and yours. If Joe is a drill sergeant and you're at boot camp, you're pretty much stuck. Ditto if he's your science teacher and you can't drop the class, or the two-year-old you agreed to babysit. If he's the slightly crazed man down the street who always yells at you for walking down the side-walk, then you have my permission to stay away. It's about station, not whether or not he likes you.

If you're in danger, like Joe is your boss who means to do you physical harm, then get away. Why? Because he's abandoned his station of boss by intend-ing to do you harm.

i messed up and made an enemy. it's my fault, and i apologized, but she won't forgive me. What do i do?

Continue to demonstrate to her you've changed your ways, if you have the opportunity. Talk is cheap; she may not believe your apology. It may be, though, she's going to hold the grudge. Then there's nothing you can do. Learn from your mistake, use it as a reminder of your need for grace, and keep going.

My dad's a pastor. He told a young couple living together they needed to repent their breaking the Sixth Commandment. Their parents are both members of the congregation, and they're furious! They've publicly said dad's not loving enough to be a pastor, and they've started a petition to force him to resign. it's horrible! What is going on?!

156

In this case, it sounds like the parents have a blind spot. Adultery is wrong in their eyes, until their own relatives are guilty. Then it's not such a bad sin anymore. When your dad stands up with the Word of God and calls sin a sin, they feel a need to protect their kids. Unfortunately, they're trying to "protect" their kids from repenting and being forgiven. They've made an idol out of their kids, who apparently can do no wrong in their sight.

This is an ugly situation. It's possible this group will succeed in pushing your dad out of his pulpit. Jesus warned this would happen:

> Blessed are you when others revile you and persecute you and utter all kinds of evil against you falsely on My account. Rejoice and be glad, for your reward is great in heaven, for so they persecuted the prophets who were before you. **(Matthew 5:11–12)**

Now, it's tough to rejoice during persecution, but Christians need to understand it confirms they are holding fast to the Word the world doesn't like.

157

If I were you, I'd pray for your dad and everyone else involved. Let him know he's doing the right thing—he could use the support. Defend the truth to others as you have the opportunity. Remember the Lord's promise, despite difficult times, "I know the plans I have for you, declares the Lord, plans for wholeness and not for evil, to give you a future and a hope" (Jeremiah 29:11).

One more thing, I'm worried about you. Throughout all this, you'll be tempted to believe the Church is beating up your dad, so you're going to want to stop going to church. If that's what you do, the devil wins again. First, he convinced some parents their feelings about their kids were more important than fol- lowing God's Word. Then, he convinced you your feelings about those parents are more important than hearing God's Word.

Don't judge the Christian Church based upon the sinners there, but upon Christ your Savior. He'll deliver you.

Your introduction to this chapter really let me off easy. Since i'm not saved by how i love my enemies, i don't have to love them, right?

Wrong. If you give yourself to hating your enemies, you spite your Savior. He's set you free from sin, including the sins of hatred and anger. If you freely indulge in hating your enemies, then you're imprisoning yourself back into sin. Your heart is going to grow cold while you dwell on your anger, think about the wrong that's been done to you, and dream about vengeance. As you dwell on your anger, you're going to want less and less to do with your Savior who has forgiveness for you . . . and your enemies.

Repent of anger toward your enemies. Give thanks the Lord died for you and them. Remember, apart from the cross, you were God's enemy (Romans 8:7) and had no hope of salvation. As He has forgiven you, so go and forgive others.

From the sounds of it in the introduction, you're saying that i shouldn't put

myself in danger to help someone else, right? is there ever a time when i should put myself at risk?

What I'm trying to tell you is you should think about your stations and abilities to serve, and then use some common sense.

As far as stations go, some stations require you to put yourself in danger; members of the armed forces, police officers, and firefighters come to mind. They're trained for such situations, so let them do the dangerous stuff when they're around. Now, if you come across a burning house with a child screaming "help" from inside and the sirens are still in the distance, you've got a decision to make. You're commanded to help your neighbor in need. You're also commanded to honor your parents, who may not be real happy you're running into burning buildings. What's the right decision, right then? I don't know—I can't know. I'll leave that to you.

As far as skills go, you might have some training that helps. If you can't swim, I wouldn't recommend helping a man who's drowning. If you do know CPR, you're better prepared to help the man in cardiac arrest than someone who doesn't—until the people with the station of "EMT" show up on the scene.

My point in the introduction has to do with common sense and dealing with enemies. I'm commanded to love my neighbor; if I don't, I sin. The problem—besides my sinful nature—is there are a lot of neighbors out there. Some of them aren't neighbors in need,

159

but criminals who want to rip me off or enemies who want to do me harm. Common sense—a gift of God!—tells me I should be careful and help those in need rather than risk my life to help those who want to hurt me. Do I sin in failing to risk my well-being? Maybe. But I'm still alive to help other people. I'm thankful I'm not saved because I helped enough people; I'm forgiven because Jesus died to help me.

162 Section Eight: Sex

Somewhere in this book, I have to write something about sex, so here goes. Actually it's easier for me to write about than to talk about, since you can't see how badly I'm turning red. Unless the editor does something cute like print this chapter in red ink. Editors. Sheesh!

Of all of God's good gifts, sex is one of the most misunderstood and misused. It's a precious gift. It's how God brings life into the world. People who reject God's plan for salvation normally just ignore the Gospel. People who reject God's plan for sex go on to abuse the gift in all sorts of ways. Misused sex soaks the culture around you, probably far more than you realize. So how are we going to tackle the topic in a short introduction? Here's an idea—let's keep in mind the four S-words from chapter 1—service, station, sin, and solution. Also Genesis 2:24, "Therefore a man shall leave his father and his mother and hold fast to his wife, and they shall become one flesh."

service

Like every other gift of God, sex is to be used in service to others. Many think this sounds stupid, but Adam and Eve were to serve by being fruitful, multiplying and filling the earth (Genesis 1:28). That's why Genesis 2:24 starts out with "therefore" there's a God-given reason for two becoming one flesh. Marriage takes place so husbands and wives serve each other as **163** comparable helpers (Genesis 2:18 NKJV), and by producing children. Back then, there were no factories turning out kids, so Adam and Eve had to make babies the old-fashioned way. Come to think of it, the only way to bring human life into the world still involves a sperm and an egg. (Cloning, you say? Nah. Cloning doesn't create new life, but makes a copy of existing life. We talked about that a little in *You Asked about Life*.) A man and woman serve one another with sex by increasing the level of intimacy between them. When a man and woman join their bodies together, there's a profound emotional bond that unites them. Sex is a matter of serving, but not between just any man and woman! God binds this sort of serving to a specific station.

station

The station is husband and wife. "Therefore a man shall leave his father and his mother and hold fast to his wife, and they shall become one flesh" (Genesis 2:24). For a variety of reasons (see the questions below), God commands sex take place only between a man and a woman who are married to one another—husband and wife. Obviously, this doesn't always happen, which is why we need to talk about sin.

sin

The sin at work here is often selfishness. Rather than use sex according to God's will, the world says you should use sex in service to yourself—for your own pride, pleasure, enjoyment, power, and so on. This doesn't mean just the act itself, because the sin begins long before. For instance, why does a girl wear tight revealing clothes leaving nothing to the imagination about her figure? Is it out of selfless concern the guys in her biology class might learn too much about cell structure and suffer a brain cramp? No. She selfishly wants the boys to give her attention. Why do the boys stare at her? Is it because they're concerned for her well-being and want to enhance her self-esteem? No. They're giving in to their coursing hormones and temptation to lust. It goes on from there.

Consider the high school couple who opt for pre-marital sex, and think of the possible reasons for them doing so. It might be they've heard so much about sex they want to satisfy their curiosity despite the sin—

that's selfishness. It might be he's sick of all the locker room jokes about his virginity, so he's willing to use a girl to get rid of the peer pressure. That's selfishness, too. It may be she's afraid if she doesn't have sex with the guy, he's going to dump her. She still wants the loser for herself as a boyfriend; or perhaps she's just learned to like the attention she gets with the guys because she's easy. Selfish!

Just about every sexual sin goes back to self-gratification, putting your own desires over the desires of others. Every sexual sin puts your own desires over God's will. All of this is included in the Sixth Commandment, "You shall not commit adultery" (Exodus 20:14). Along with adultery, God also condemns "sexual intercourse between unmarried persons . . . , rape, homosexual activity, incest, sexual child abuse, obscenity, and the use of pornographic materials" (SC, pages 82–83), as the explanation to the Small Catechism says. If it's not consensual sexual activity between a husband and wife, it's out-of-bounds sin.

Just in case you think you've been doing a great job keeping the Sixth Commandment, you'll be just thrilled to know this also includes impure sexual thoughts. Jesus says, "You have heard that it was said, 'You shall not commit adultery.' But I say to you that everyone who looks at a woman with lustful intent has already committed adultery with her in his heart" (Matthew 5:27–28). Does the Lord take this seriously? Look at the next few verses:

> If your right eye causes you to sin, tear
> it out and throw it away. For it is bet-

165

> ter that you lose one of your members than that your whole body be thrown into hell. And if your right hand causes you to sin, cut it off and throw it away. For it is better that you lose one of your members than that your whole body go into hell. **(Matthew 5:29–30)**

Yup! The Lord takes this seriously. But before you get out the machete, read about the solution.

solution

On His way to the cross, Jesus lived a perfectly pure life in thought, word and deed. Where you're tempted to use your looks and dance moves to get all kinds of wrong attention, Jesus became flesh who "had no form or majesty that we should look at Him, and no beauty that we should desire Him" (Isaiah 53:2). Because you want to use your body for sinful pleasure, He allowed His to be shredded by a scourge and nailed to a cross. Where your mind wants to spend way too much time fantasizing about lust, He continued to focus on a single, painful prayer, "My Father, if it be possible, let this cup pass from Me; nevertheless, not as I will, but as You will" (Matthew 26:39). He self-lessly suffered and died for your sins, so you could be forgiven. Don't try to make yourself pure by cutting off your right hand. It's already too late. Instead, confess your sins and be forgiven. So powerful is His forgiveness, no matter what you've done, by His final Word you are pure and holy once again.

Q & A:
You Ask . . .

167

...or you were
afraid to

There's a couple in youth group who are having sex. They say God understands, so it's okay. is it?

Nope. The question to ask is, "How do you know it's okay with God?" I'll almost guarantee the answer is based on emotion, the whole thing "feels" right. But can they show from Scripture where God permits fornication? No. They're fooling themselves and destroying their faith.

My older brother moved in with his girlfriend. He said they intend to get married, but they just can't afford it right now. How do you answer?

168

I hear this one a lot when I'm talking to couples who are living together because of "economic necessity." Apparently, money is so tight there was no way to survive without committing immorality. They couldn't live with their parents or find a roommate for a while. Furthermore, that $50 marriage license at the courthouse was too much on top of the apartment, two new cars and plasma television. It was move in and have sex or go bankrupt.

Oh, please! The "economic necessity" argument is using poverty as an excuse to break God's law. God doesn't permit this in the Bible. This couple is saying sex and money are more important than the Lord.

is masturbation a sin?

We've already said that the main sin regarding sex is selfishness. Masturbation means stimulating your own body for your own sexual pleasure. That sounds pretty self-centered to me. It's also usually accompanied by sinful thoughts of lust, so you've polluted your mind before you've ever gotten around to your body. It's not as dangerous as premarital sex, but it's still sinful.

Why is pornography wrong? it's not like the models don't want to be seen.

It's wrong because you're using pictures of peoples' bodies to fill your mind with lustful thoughts. That's selfishness on your part, using them and defying God's command to flee from lust (2 Timothy 2:22). Fleeing is a good idea. The more you fill your mind with pornographic garbage, the more warped your view of sex, love, and other people. Furthermore, this will seriously hurt your chances of a happy life and lead you to more dangerous activities. Using porn isn't a static activity. If you start out using the soft-core stuff, it's only a matter of time until your sinful flesh wants something a little more graphic, then a little more . . . . If you really want to be miserable and lost, this is a great way to do it.

169

i can't stop thinking about sex, and i'm not sure i want to. What do i do?

Here's the question back—what are you filling your mind with? Between television, the Internet, and conversation by the lockers at school, your day might be filled with sexual suggestions. If that's what's going into your mind a lot, then what do you suppose you'll be thinking about a lot? Here's what you do:

> Finally, brothers, whatever is true, whatever is honorable, whatever is just, whatever is pure, whatever is lovely, whatever is commendable, if there is any excellence, if there is anything worthy of praise, think about these things. **(Philippians 4:8)**

170 Fill up your mind with pure things to think about. Memorize portions of the Bible, like Romans 6 or Psalm 34. When your mind starts to wander, start reciting the Small Catechism in your head. Pray the Lord's Prayer.

When your mind starts wandering back to impure thoughts, don't entertain them, confess them as sin. Give thanks for forgiveness, and rejoice you're set free to think about pure things again.

How far is "too far" on a date?

I hate this question, because it sounds like you want to know what line you can sprint to before God gets mad. I'm not going to give you an easy answer. Here are some things to think about.

First: Obviously, sexual intercourse before marriage is "too far."

Second: Physical affection progresses in a relationship, and it's progressing toward sex. The longer you go out with someone, the more affectionate you want to be.

Third: The more affectionate you get, the fewer steps are left between where you are and going too far.

Fourth: The more affection you show now, the less you have reserved only for your future spouse.

Fifth: You don't owe your casual date any sort of physical affection. You *do* owe your future spouse faithfulness and virginity. The more you save up for the one you marry, the better the relationship will be in marriage.

171

Given that, take things slow. Real slow! Instead of asking, "How far can I go now?" I'd be thinking, "How much can I save for the one I'm going to spend my life with?"

What is "hooking up" or "friends with benefits"?

These are terms that describe casual sexual relationships. Really casual! As in a boy and girl meet at a party and "hook up" for the rest of the night. Or a couple has a nominal friendship, but they keep sleeping with each other for sexual gratification.

By the time this book is published, there will be new expressions to describe the same old sins. These terms are popular because they sound so much better than "fornication," since "fornication" sounds so . . . so ugly and sinful. Whatever you call it, that's what it is.

is formication wrong?

No!

172

Huh?

Formication is the sensation ants are crawling on you, when they really aren't. I just happened to find this one in the dictionary today and wanted to pass it on. Isn't your life just that much richer now? However, fornication—sexual immorality—is most certainly sinful and contrary to God's Word.

My friends say that it's good to be faithful once you're married, but you should "play the field" while you're single so you can bring some experience into marriage. What do you say?

Which experiences do they hope to bring into marriage? The experience of dealing with permanent sexually transmitted diseases? The experience of cheapening sex so it really doesn't mean much in marriage? The message to their spouse they've been happy to fool around with different people before, so why should it change now? The ability to compare their spouse's lovemaking with another person's? How romantic! None of this is going to help their marriage in the slightest. It's going to do it a lot of damage.

if you're going to be married to someone for the rest of your life, shouldn't you make sure you get along sexually? As the world says, what about a "test drive" before marriage?

173

Ah, the good old "test drive" argument to justify premarital sex. Let's take a look at a couple of scenarios.

If you give the "test drive" theory some thought, it suggests a couple will only fornicate when they're just about to get married. It's like this is the last thing on the checklist before they buy the ring. Therefore, it's logical to assume the two are virgins who just want to make sure that their sex life is going to be okay. So, they do it. But because they're both inexperienced, it goes terribly. Now, if they were doing this because it was going to decide whether or not to marry, they've got a problem. It went badly, so they'd better break off the relationship . . . or take the car out for another spin. Look at that! Another excuse for sin! In the midst of all of this, they now have added anxiety, guilt, and anger. Gee, this idea sure worked well for making them feel better about their upcoming marriage.

Of course, the virgin scenario isn't the only way the world sees it. The world has both emphasized and diminished sex to the point where some would say you should have sex on the first date to see if the relationship is worth pursuing. If you buy into this theory, then sex is essentially meaningless by the time the wedding night rolls around.

Look, the "test drive" argument is just another sinful ploy to try to justify premarital sex. As you'll see in the next chapter, marriage is about a husband and wife serving each other in all aspects of life. Build a marriage on sex alone, and it's going to die. Build a marriage on mutual serving in all areas, and the marriage is going to be strong. So, by the way, is the sex.

Aw, but what about "free love," man? Waiting until marriage for sex means there are a lot of strings attached.

"Free love, man?" Thanks for taking us back to the sixties. But anyway, another great euphemism for fornication is "free love" or "loving freely." Let's talk about this. In this world, what sorts of things are normally free? Things that have no worth! What sorts of things aren't free? Things that have value.

When someone engages in "free love," they're giv-

174

ing away their body and emotions for free. What does this say about them? They're not worth much. In fact, promiscuous people often feel worthless. People seem to appreciate them only for certain body parts and availability. Sadly, when they sense this feeling of worthlessness, they may actually become more promiscuous—the downward spiral continues.

You're not worth nothing, remember? You're priceless. God redeemed you at the cost of His Son's priceless blood. Furthermore, He values your body so highly that He says your lover must commit to a lifetime of mutual service in marriage first. Free love cheapens you to the point of worthlessness. All those "strings" that come with marriage (like a lifetime commitment to love, honor, have, hold, etc.) indicate how much the Lord values you and His gift of sexuality.

175

When Jesus warns against lust and says, "if your right eye causes you to sin, tear it out and throw it away" (Matthew 5:29), He was only kidding, right?

The passage actually reads:

> If your right eye causes you to sin, tear it out and throw it away. For it is better that you lose one of your members than that your whole body be thrown into hell. And if your right hand causes you to sin, cut it off and throw it away. For it is better that you lose one of your members than that your whole body go into hell. **(Matthew 5:29–30)**

God's not kidding. I mean, it would be better to spend life here missing an eye or a hand than to spend eternity in hell, wouldn't it? But remember, He's preaching the Law. He's showing people how futile it is to trust in their purity to get themselves to heaven. If a guy takes out his right eye because he lusts with it, is he free of lust? No. He'll have to remove his left eye within a few days. If he cuts off his right hand because he's using it to access porn on the Web, is he sin-free? Nope. He'll have to take the axe to his left hand, too. Jesus is trying tell you how futile it is to make yourself pure by your own actions.

So when you sin, don't start hacking off limbs or gouging eyes; you'll still be sinful. Instead, confess the sin, be forgiven, and make better use of your hands and eyes.

176

is oral sex really sex?

I debated a long time before including this question, since it seems so obvious. But recent polls indicate over half of all teens in the United States have engaged in oral sex, so I guess we better discuss the question.

From a strictly vocabulary standpoint, let's give this some thought. It's called oral sex. It's not called oral *notsex*. Wow, that was a tough one to think through. So when someone asks the question, it usually means they're trying to find a loophole to do something they want to do, even though they know they shouldn't.

Some want to argue you can engage in oral sex and still be a virgin. They contend as long as you haven't actually had sexual intercourse, you've kept your virginity. Therefore, oral sex is just as innocent as, say, holding hands or kissing. This is called the "technical virginity" argument, as in "I'm still technically a virgin, even though I've been engaging in activities with people that give us sexual excitement." Yes, some people actually believe this is a good argument!

A lot of doctors have a different view. Whether you've "technically" had intercourse or not, oral sex still makes it really easy for you to contract all sorts of sexually transmitted diseases that can hurt you for life—or kill you. From a disease transmission standpoint, oral sex is just like having full intercourse with someone—and with everyone else they've ever had (oral) sex with.

177

So, here's my answer—duh!

Yes, it's sex. Now, you can whine away about the "technical virginity" argument and say, "By my definition, it's not." In that case, I'll say, "Ok, then it's not by your (self-serving) definition." But it is still sin. It's still moral impurity, as much as sexual intercourse before marriage. If you think you can use your mouth on the genitals of someone else for sexual pleasure now, or vice versa, and still consider yourself not sexually active, you're lying to yourself. Even if you maintain your "technical virginity" until your wedding night, your marriage will never be as intimate as it could have been, because you can't even admit how pure you're not.

What are the chances of contracting a sexually transmitted disease?

If you search the Web, you'll find that the oft-repeated statistic is one in four teenagers will contract an STD this year. One in four! It doesn't say one in four sexually active teens, but 25% of all teens! If you want more happy news, half of all 25-year-olds will have contracted at least one STD. Half! That's a pretty big chunk of the dating pool.

Now, consider a few more things:

* These diseases aren't like a common cold that goes away in a few days. A lot of them are incurable, so you have to deal with the disease and the symptoms for life, including itching, burning, oozing, and warts in all the wrong places. A lot of sexually transmitted diseases cause infertility. Many young women have no idea they've contracted Chlamydia, and years later they will find out they can never have children. Keep this in mind; some of these diseases will kill you, even when treatments are available.

* What are your chances of getting a sexually transmitted disease if you're not having sex? Pretty much zero.

* What are your chances of contracting an STD if you're a virgin who marries a virgin? Again, you're down there at zero.

* Here's a question for you: given the fact 25% of

the dating pool has an STD in high school already, do you think keeping higher standards is important?

is homosexuality a sin?

Homosexuality is a sin. Why? Because the Lord says so in His Word. Among other places, Romans 1:26–27 makes this clear, as does 1 Corinthians 6:9.

Some people argue that St. Paul wrote both of those texts, and he was a homophobe who hated gays. is this true?

179

No, and no! Paul didn't write these texts. While he might be the guy with the pen, God was the author. Those who argue Paul wrote these because he was homophobic are betraying themselves; they're admitting they don't believe the Bible is God's Word.

Furthermore, to speak the truth is neither phobic nor hateful. God gives His Law to show people their sin, their need for repentance and forgiveness Jesus died to give them.

But hasn't science proven homosexuality is genetic—just like heterosexuality?

Based upon research, some scientists claim homosexuality is genetic. In other words, people who are gay are simply "born that way." Other scientists have conducted studies and concluded homosexuality is not genetic, but strictly a learned behavior. The debate will continue.

From the standpoint of a doctor or a psychologist, this might be important information. Here's a question from this pastor's perspective—so what? Why does it matter whether homosexuality is genetic or not?

What I mean is this, there's an agenda behind this debate. Those who seek to prove homosexuality is genetic do so to prove that homosexuality is natural; and if it's natural, they say, it can't be wrong.

So let's try this out scientifically. There is no doubt about it among scientists: sickle cell anemia is genetic. It's all in the chromosomes. Therefore, sickle cell anemia is natural and can't be wrong.

See my point? This world is soaked in sin. Sin even corrupts your health at the level of genes and DNA. Therefore, even if homosexuality were genetic (and I'm not ready to say it is), that doesn't mean it's okay and acceptable to God.

Let's try out a moral example. I'm going to make the shocking observation that heterosexual men are predisposed to lust after women to whom they're not married. (No, no! you argue; they just watch all that sleazy television in order to support the sponsors, who are really doing humanitarian work around the world.) If this is true, does it make heterosexual lust acceptable to God? Hardly! Jesus calls it adultery (Matthew 5:28).

So how do i deal with homosexuals?

How do you deal with anybody who is sinful? As a Christian, you'll interact with all sorts of people every day. As you do so, you seek to give a good witness in your actions and words. You don't mock people for their sin or shun them. On the other hand, you don't encourage them in their sin, indicate it's a good thing or participate in it. While homosexuality is a sin that still has a pretty strong stigma attached, it is given to you and me to act as Christians and to speak the truth in love as the opportunity arises. Give 1 Corinthians 5:9–13 a good read. In this section of Scripture St. Paul declares we should never sanction immorality among Christians. In fact we should shun those who claim to be Christian and yet support immorality. **181** However, he doesn't tell us to shun non-Christians who suffer from such sins; instead, he says you and I will interact with them on a daily basis.

What if i think i'm gay?

This question really lies outside of the scope of a little book like this. But I'll offer the following advice.

First, seek out the advice of a trusted, Christian adult. Your parents are always the right first choice; however, I can understand why you may not consider it to be the case here. Your pastor would be the next one on my list; we're pretty good at being discreet.

Now, chances are your pastor doesn't hold a degree in counseling; if he doesn't and he's smart, he may look to refer you to a good Christian counselor. This is important, because different counselors have different ideas. Some say homosexuality is okay, they'll seek to help you accept it as a good thing. A Christian counselor should see homosexuality as a sin and seek to help you out of it.

The other reason to speak with your pastor is this; counseling doesn't get rid of sin. Forgiveness does, and it's the pastor's calling to declare to you Christ died for all of your sins. Some sins carry greater shame than others, but the Lord died for them all. Seek out your pastor to hear absolution.

182 How come guys are expected to sleep around, and girls are expected to be virgins until their wedding night? is this a double standard? is it fair?

It is a double standard, and it's not fair; but it's still largely true.

Just take a look at clothing. Every year brings a new wave of fashions for girls designed to show off their bodies and make them look sexy. On the other hand, the biggest innovation for guys seems to be oversized jeans that keep falling down. If you look at couples on dates, the girls are usually dressed up while the guys have thoughtfully put on a clean(er) T-shirt for the evening. Girls are expected to dress to look sexually inviting; guys are just expected to be dressed.

Guys are usually praised for scoring, as if sex is a

football game, while girls are usually respected for a strong defense. While guys might want to go out with easy girls, they don't respect them—and they sure don't want to marry them. Rest assured this double standard is a product of the world. It's also disappearing. Feminist groups and others have insisted on an end to the double standard, on a woman's right to revel in immorality. Many polls indicate young women are becoming as crass and immoral as their male counterparts. Personally, I'm not sure civilization can last much longer.

The Lord calls for the end of the double standard, as well. He demands both men and women wait until marriage. The alarming numbers of sexually active teens today indicate how much the world has rejected His Word.

183

i can't believe it! After we went out for a few weeks (months), i actually let a guy talk me into having sex. Now he won't even talk to me—but he's told all his buddies. The whole school knows! i feel so ashamed. What can i do?

There are a number of things to address here. First off, keep in mind guys who are willing to violate your virginity for their own personal satisfaction are also willing to lie to you. Whatever line he used to persuade you, he didn't mean it. It was a con. That's probably why he won't talk to you now. He's a loser who got what he wanted, and now he wants to move on. You, on the other hand, gave him a gift . . . and because you entrusted him with something so precious, you still want him around.

This is going to hurt badly, so be careful how you react. Dump him now. You want a better guy than this anyway; and the more you pursue him, the more he's likely to spread the word about his "conquest" to make you miserable. The sooner this fades away in peoples' minds, the better.

Beware of a couple of common trends. One is self-destructive promiscuity. You might be so angry at yourself or feel so worthless, you become sexually active to punish yourself or try to feel "loved." That's only going to make things worse. Watch out for depression, too. You're going to be mad at him, and you're going to be mad at yourself. If you hold all of this anger in, depression is likely to occur. Find a trusted adult and talk it out.

Even better, go to your pastor for private confession and absolution. Believe me, he's heard a lot worse confessions from other people in the congregation. Not only can you talk it out in a confidential environment, but he can also declare you forgiven. From the sound of your question, you're going to feel ashamed for a while. What's going to get you through this time is the assurance Jesus has already taken your guilt away.

What about me?
i've been sexually abused.

Sexual abuse—incest, rape, date-rape, and the

like—is one of the most repulsive violent acts. The sad
fact is it's relatively common in this world. A quick
check of the local sheriff's Web site reveals sixty-two
registered sex offenders in my zip code alone. That's
just the ones who have been caught and convicted.

Sex abuse is especially vile for a number of reasons. Earlier we said the principal sin was usually selfishness? In sexual abuse, the offender is so obsessive-
ly selfish that he wants to violate others to feed his
own feelings of power—not pleasure, but power. The
offender is almost always a man—that's why the few
female offenders make the big splash in the news.
Now, when he's already that selfish, he's going to
believe that (a) the assault isn't wrong, and/or (b) if it
is wrong, then it must be the victim's fault, since it
can't be his. Think of the idiot high school guy who
assaults his date and says afterwards, "You wanted it!"
or the rapist on trial who claims the crime happened
because the woman was dressed provocatively.
Abusive adults have been known to tell their child victims they must endure the abuse as part of honoring
authorities—when in fact the adults have abandoned
their station as authorities to be honored, and should
instead be regarded as criminals to be jailed.

The consequences for victims are many. Victims
often believe the assault is their fault, taking responsibility for the offender's sin. Since God designed sex to
build trust between people for life, a sexual assault is
going to destroy the victim's ability to trust others for
a long time. Furthermore, the feelings of being violated are crushing. If you are a victim, you'll feel like the

185

offender did more than violate your body. You'll feel like he killed your soul. The devil wants to make you feel as worthless and distant from God as possible, which is why he delights in sexual abuse. Victims can expect to battle depression, perhaps even suicidal thoughts.

Is there hope? Absolutely! Look, I'm a pastor, not a trained counselor, so helping you with a lot of the recovery lies outside of my training. But I'll tell you what I do know. First, you should report the assault to an adult whom you trust, no matter who assaulted you. Second, a good counselor can help you a lot.

Third, and this part does lie in my calling, know this: no matter how you feel, the abuser didn't get anywhere close to killing your soul. At your Baptism, Jesus joined you to His death and resurrection. He's already given your soul eternal life. At His trial and on the cross, man horribly abused the Lord. Just as His body was not off-limits to suffering, neither are His peoples'. But as He was raised from the dead, fully restored, He lives fully to restore you. Where you feel cut off from God and dead in your soul, cling to His Word, "Fear not, for I have redeemed you; I have called you by name, you are mine" (Isaiah 43:1). No matter what someone evil does to you, no one can snatch you out of the Lord's hand.

Way back in chapter 2, I mentioned the greatest treasures in this world often receive the least amount of praise. This is most certainly true when it comes to virginity and sex according to God's commands. The world likes to tell you the Church condemns sex, which just goes to show you how the world gets it all wrong again. Christians don't condemn sex; they want to preserve it the way God wants it to be. I want you to make use of your sexuality in the way that pleases God and benefits you. Setting aside the pressures of society and coursing hormones for a second, which sounds better?

> A series of short sexual relationships where you risk disease and death, and wear down your ability to truly love someone while you battle feelings of depression and wonder why you feel so empty.

> Or, a lifelong, faithful relationship with one other person where you're always seeking to make each other happy.

187

Forget what the world says. The world is going to hell. If you're still a virgin, give thanks to God and save the treasure for someone who's willing to commit to you for life. If you've engaged in immorality, confess the sin to God and be forgiven. Be set free from sin, and know the Lord sees you as pure and holy, without spot or blemish or any such thing. That forgiveness in Christ is the greatest treasure of all.

188 Section Nine: Dating and More Serious Relationships

Sooner or later, you start thinking about dating, about spending time with persons of the opposite sex. It may be that you're thinking *sooner*, while your parents are thinking *later*. The prospect of going out on a date starts to sound like a good idea. In our culture today, dating is seen as a fundamental right, like breathing or television. I mean, how could it be any other way?

Dating is trickier than you might think, so what I want to do is start out by making sure we're on the same wavelength with the facets of service, station, sin, and solution. We'd better start out with your station first; in other words, what's the purpose of dating? You won't find a chapter of dating tips in the Bible, so we're going to have to use some common sense. Stick with me here, and we'll see if we can track through this.

What's the real purpose of dating?

To have fun? You can have fun on a date, but you can also have fun not on a date, with friends of the same sex. Having fun is not a purpose unique to dating. Common interests? Again, both of you might enjoy comparing the prices of kitchenware at local stores. (In which case, you'll write to the publisher and demand they publish my latest book *You Ask about Spatulas*.) But once again you can do this with friends while not on a date. There's something about dating that puts it in a class by itself.

So why go out on a date? Because you're attracted to someone of the opposite sex, and you want to spend time with them?

Ah, now we're getting somewhere. Logically, you don't want to spend time with people that you find repulsive or boring, right? You want to go out with someone you find attractive, entertaining, enchanting, and so forth. You hope they find you attractive, too. Be honest; that's really what dating is about.

Next question: Where is a dating relationship headed? More than any other relationship, this one is volatile. It's always changing, and people are usually on edge as to what's going to happen next. Dating relationships aren't usually static or stable. They're either getting more serious; heading for a breakup; or new enough so nobody has any idea what's going on yet but it's a fun ride so far. This leaves the people who are dating either nervous wrecks or so annoyingly happy that life is especially wonderful, the birds are singing and the grout in the shower looked extra sparkly this morning. Ah, the mysteries of love!

Now, if a relationship breaks up, then it's over. But if it gets more serious, where does it go next? Every facet is going to get deeper. The couple grows closer as they share more stories and thoughts. They'll adapt themselves to help out the other; they'll eventually become emotionally entwined. They'll be more attracted to each other physically, as well. It's a package deal. Eventually, the couple has to make a decision: is this serious relationship going to end, or is it going to keep on getting more intimate? If you try for something in between it's going to stagnate and die. In other words, are they going to break it off, or are they going to get married?

Does this line of thinking make sense?

If it does, then here's something to keep in mind whenever you go on a date. When you date, you're inviting the possibility of a relationship—maybe a serious one. The most serious relationship is marriage. So when you date, your station is the station of "potential husband or wife."

No way, right? You're thinking about maybe going with someone to dinner and a school dance, definitely not about marriage. I've got to be nuts. If that's the case, then let's work this backwards.

Take your typical married couple. How did they get to know each other before they got married? They were dating first. People don't marry everyone they date; but just about every husband or wife has married someone they've dated. Very few have married a complete stranger or someone they ran into at the produce department twice. A lot of their stories will include the phrase, "When we first met, I never dreamed he/she was the one. . . ." Every dating relationship is a potential for marriage. That means your station is "potential husband or wife."

191

This also means whoever you're dating has the station of your "potential spouse."

Yup, even in high school. High school sweethearts sometimes get married.

Kind of scary, isn't it?

If we've got the station down, then we can move on to service. What sort of serving are you given to do when you're dating? Again, we're going to work backwards. How were Adam and Eve supposed to treat each other? They were to serve one another, putting the other first, according to God's will. That's still how marriage is supposed to work today—a life of mutual service. Ephesians 5:22–27 describes things nicely:

> Wives, submit to your own husbands,
> as to the Lord. For the husband is the
> head of the wife even as Christ is the
> head of the church, His body, and is
> Himself its Savior. Now as the church
> submits to Christ, so also wives should
> submit in everything to their hus-
> bands. Husbands, love your wives, as
> Christ loved the church and gave
> Himself up for her, that He might
> sanctify her, having cleansed her by
> the washing of water with the Word,
> so that He might present the church
> to Himself in splendor, without spot or
> wrinkle or any such thing, that she
> might be holy and without blemish.

192

Wives are to submit to husbands as the Church sub-
mits to Christ. As the Church prays to Jesus, "Thy will
be done," so the wife says, "I'm here to serve you, not
work to get my own way." As Jesus loved the Church,
so the husband says, "I'm here for your welfare, even
to the point of death." That's the hard work of mutual
service and submission that keep a marriage going . . .
even when the other is being a brat.

You're not married yet, so you're not quite bound
to this yet. However, if you're a potential spouse dating a potential spouse, you've got a twofold task. The
first is to put the other first, always according to the
Word of God. The second is to examine the other person and see what kind of a servant he or she is. If
you're dating someone who's selfish, who always
demands to be served, get out now! This also means

that if someone demands you serve in a way that disobeys God's Word, you say no. If you're dating someone who looks out for you, too, then there's potential there for more.

So what's the sin? The sin is selfishness, desiring to get your own way. Like going out with someone because they have a lot of money and spend it freely. Like ignoring your parents' curfew because you want to do something else. Like getting way too physical, way too fast, because it feels good and it makes your date more interested in you. There are all sorts of ways to be selfish while you're dating. But understand what you're doing: you're training yourself to use other people for your own satisfaction, and that's lousy training if you're planning on marriage someday. Furthermore, when the relationship is feeding you all sorts of good feelings and emotions, it's easy to set aside God's Word for what you want, and that's some real dangerous selfishness because you're saying you'll put your own desires over God's commands when it comes to the most serious of matters.

193

What's the solution? Jesus, of course! Reread Ephesians 5:22–27 then note what St. Paul says five verses later, "This mystery is profound, and I am saying that it refers to Christ and the church" (Ephesians 5:32). St. Paul is talking about marriage, but he's speaking more of how much Jesus loves you. In loving service to you, He gave Himself up to the cross to sanctify and cleanse you, to make you part of His Church—His bride—for eternal life. Even though you're sinful—and can be a real jerk—the Lord in His love forgives you. His love sets you free to love others (1 John 4:19). More importantly, His faithfulness as a bridegroom to you guarantees—no matter how other relationships go—He will never leave you nor forsake you.

Q & A:
You Ask . . .

195

i've found that it's a lot easier to get a date if i'm willing to spend a lot of money on the girl. is this good or bad?

I enjoyed spending money on my future wife when we were dating. Sometimes I'd even let her get a Big Mac, even if I didn't have a coupon with me. But a good date doesn't have to cost much. I think most dates shouldn't cost much. There's a difference between treating a girl to a nice time and renting her company by spending a lot of money. Healthy relationships are built on common interests, values and standards. Are you spending money to be nice, or to hide who you really are? Don't try to buy companionship.

If she will only go out with you because you spend a lot of money on her, then I'd counsel you not to ask her out again.

A guy just asked me out on a date to a really expensive restaurant. Should this tell me anything?

It should tell you one of several things. It may mean he's a really nice guy who wants to treat you to a nice meal. It may also mean that he hasn't checked the prices on the menu, so you might be washing dishes before the hostess will give you your coat back.

However, keep in mind the old proverb "there's no such thing as a free lunch." Sadly, there are a lot of guys out there who aren't thinking about giving freely, but trading. As in, "If I take her out for a nice dinner, then she owes me . . ." The sentence usually ends with something involving sex.

196

Before you go out with the guy, check him out. Does he have a good reputation? Has he gone through a lot of girls who now thoroughly hate him? Be careful.

Sometimes, a real creepy guy asks me out. How can i discourage him?

One great strategy is to arrange with your folks so all your dates, creepy or not, have to call them—preferably your dad—and ask for permission to take

you out. I'll guarantee this will thin the number of losers who ask you out.

Even more, remember who you are, a redeemed
child of God, set free from sin to live by His Word.
Keep those standards high and say no. You don't have
to go out with someone because they asked. Don't date
to be nice to somebody lonely. Be nice to them outside
of dating. Remember, your station in dating is potential spouse.

i just got asked to a dance, but my parents don't look happy. He's African-American, and i'm white. is interracial dating wrong?

197

I can't find anything in the Bible against interracial
dating—or marriage for that matter. I mean, you have
a verse like 1 Kings 11:1–2:

> Now King Solomon loved many for-
> eign women, along with the daughter
> of Pharaoh: Moabite, Ammonite,
> Edomite, Sidonian, and Hittite women,
> from the nations concerning which
> the Lord had said to the people of
> Israel, "You shall not enter into mar-
> riage with them, neither shall they
> with you, for surely they will turn away
> your heart after their gods." Solomon
> clung to these in love.

However, the reason for this prohibition in the Old
Testament was primarily religious, not racial. Each

nation had its own gods, and so the Lord warned, "surely they will turn away your heart after their gods." In the New Testament, Jesus doesn't renew this commandment; but He does make clear He died to redeem people of all nations (Matthew 28:19; Revelation 14:6).

So where does the idea interracial dating is wrong come from? It comes from the opinions of man, either a rank prejudice or an ingrained feeling of "it's just not right." Really, widespread interracial dating is something relatively new in the United States, largely unheard of when your parents were starting to date. If I were you, I'd talk to your parents about what makes them feel so uneasy. If I were your parents, I'd pray more you date a faithful Christian than someone of the same skin color.

All the same, be aware there are a lot of people who still oppose interracial relationships, so don't be surprised if you catch some flack. Then again, part of serving one another is defending the other against untrue criticism and prejudice.

i met this guy, and he's just like nobody else. i mean, the way he just, you know, makes me feel when he's around? Ooh! Ooh! Dougie's like, oh i don't know, you know?

Honestly, I don't have the slightest idea what you are talking about.

i don't get asked out on dates very much. Why am i not popular?

That's tough to answer without knowing you better, but I'll take this opportunity to share a universal truth. The higher your standards, the fewer dates you have. Let's say you have no standards, you'll go out with anyone and do whatever they want you to do. You're going to get a bunch of invitations—mostly from losers who want a cheap thrill or to spend someone else's money. People with high standards don't ask people with low standards out on a date. It's part of having high standards. On the other hand, if—for instance—you're a girl who says, "I will only date guys who are six feet tall with curly blond hair and blue eyes, named "Wellington" and enjoy making sculptures out of corn chips," then you've cut your dating pool down to just about nobody; so, you shouldn't expect too many dates, especially since all the good chip sculptors are already taken. See? The higher the standards, the fewer the dates.

Listen to me carefully. It is far better to have high standards than a lot of dates. Never forget, any dating relationship could lead to marriage.

So even if i haven't been on a date yet, i'm okay?

Yea and amen! The higher your standards, the fewer the dates you'll have. As a teacher of mine once said unkindly about a girl in my class, "She gets taken out once a week. Just like the trash."

How do i establish standards?

I'll give you two sources for standards. Believe it or not, you've got a good start with the Ten Commandments. If God commands you to honor His Word (Third Commandment), speak well of others (Eighth Commandment) and practice moral purity (Sixth Commandment), then you should only date those who desire to honor God's Word, speak well of others and practice sexual purity. Even though sinners can't keep the Law perfectly, you've been set free from sin to follow His commands. You should date others who regard His Word in the same way.

200

The other good source is your parents. If they're at all involved in your life, then you're going to have to work with them on dating. Talk to them about their expectations for you and your date.

I s'pose, too, if you read through all the questions in this book, you'll get a few more tips on standards.

You said dating was based on attraction. But don't some people date out of peer pressure or desperation, because someone finally asked them out?

Yup, and it's not a particularly good thing. Going out because you feel peer pressure says, "I'm willing to lower my standards because I'm afraid of what other people think of me." Going out because of desperation says, "I'm willing to lower my standards just because I want to say I've been on a date." The one who's asking may be expecting you to lower your standards, just because you've been asked out. Don't do it. Stick to your standards. Be patient. Your worth doesn't come from how many dates you have. Your worth comes from the unchangeable truth that Christ died to redeem you.

i've got a serious crush on this girl. is that good or bad?

A crush is a crush; it's not necessarily good or bad. It's also called an infatuation, which is often defined in dictionaries using words like "foolish" and "affection." It's when you just can't stop thinking about that special someone. You draw art with their name in the middle and you start composing bad poetry about how fascinating you find their eyelashes and the enchanting way they hold their pencil during math class. It's that wonderful feeling of being "in love."

But it's a feeling. Emotions change. A crush feels great when a relationship goes well. It leaves you tied up in knots when the object of your affection doesn't seem to notice you. And it hurts badly if you get rejected.

Furthermore, emotions don't last. Not only do a lot of people start dating because they're infatuated, but they also get married because they're infatuated.

201

They've convinced themselves they're always, always, always going to feel the same way about each other. Know how long those feelings last? Two years, maybe! Which leaves only 50–60 more years of married life ahead. At this point, a lot of couples get a divorce because they don't feel like they're in love anymore.

So here are the dangers of a crush. First, as an emotion, it's a pretty selfish emotion: an infatuation makes you want to be with someone because of how they make you feel. You're not acting as a servant, but as one who wants attention. Second, emotions can make you relax your standards, even though you know better. (You know better than to throw a punch, but a feeling of anger can make you do it anyway. You know better than to start heavy petting on a date, but . . .) Third, a crush isn't love. Remember; love is hard work. Crushes go away. The love produced by the hard work of serving one another doesn't.

202

i met this girl, and wow. She's got this way, well, i can't stop thinking about her. i mean, uh, i get all funny-feeling. You know?

Not really. But, just by chance, is your name Dougie? No matter how nice she is, stop sending me your poetry. "Geometry" and "go with me" don't really rhyme, anyway.

QA: DATING AND MORE SERIOUS RELATIONSHIPS

How old should i be before i start dating?

Thirty-two!

Seriously, there's no magic number. When you start to date is not determined by the calendar, it's determined by your maturity, your parents, and their trust in you. Don't groan, this is part of the Fourth Commandment. There's a good chance they won't be quite as anxious for you to start dating as you are. Not necessarily because of you, but because of whoever might ask you out. Talk with your parents about when they think you should date, what events are appropriate, curfews, and so forth. Set the standards with them. Here's another clue, the more you honor your parents and act responsibly, the more they're going to trust you to make the right decisions when you're out of the house.

203

Speaking of parents, my girlfriend's parents are obnoxious! Do i have to honor them?

Right now, you honor your girlfriend's parents in order to honor her. If the two of you get married, then they're your parents, too. In the meantime, remember, people learn how to act from their parents. Just like you've picked up a lot of your parents' habits (good and bad), so has she. You can learn a lot about your girlfriend by interacting with her parents.

Can i "just be friends" with a member of the opposite sex?

It's possible to just be friends, especially if you haven't dated. If you already have a dating history, it's not going to work. The longer you've dated each other, the more this is true.

So it's possible to be just friends, but this type of friendship isn't necessarily completely stable. It's likely to be temporary. For one thing, the more time friends spend together, the more they serve each other and get to know each other, the more the friendship deepens. There's a pretty good chance, sooner or later, one of you is going to want more of a dating relationship and less than a friendship. This may lead to a life-long marriage, or it may lead to the end of the friendship. For another, if either of you gets into a serious dating relationship with someone else, your friendship is going to weaken dramatically.

My advice, friends can be honest with each other. Make sure each of you know each other's ideas and limits on the friendship, and make sure you act according to God's Word. (See the idiotic subject of "friends with benefits" in the chapter on sex.)

is it true opposites attract, and is this a good thing?

Opposites attract and do quite well in a variety of ways. An obvious example is a couple where one likes to talk all the time and the other seldom says anything.

They've found a good match, since one enjoys talking and the other listening. Another example might be where one is a daredevil and the other is cautious. The first appreciates the restraint of the second, while the second likes the sense of adventure the first brings along. One who is outgoing is often attracted to one who is shy. They balance each other well. So yes, opposites attract, and those opposites can often really complement each other.

Some opposites can be difficult to deal with. For instance, if one comes from a wealthy background and the other from a poor setting, they'll probably have a tough time fitting into each other's worlds. If they're from different cultures, the same rule applies. Should it be that way? Doesn't matter, it is that way!

Furthermore, opposites are not a good thing when it comes to standards, values, and faith. If one believes relationships are about serving while the other believes they're about being selfish, it's going to go badly. If one believes in premarital sex and the other doesn't, there's going to be anger and grief. If one is a Christian and the other is not, then one will seek to honor the Lord while the other does not.

Should i only date Christians?

Here's a question which shows how much it pays to look ahead at the rest of your life. I'm going to say up front it's best to marry someone of the same faith with the following Bible verse in mind, "Do not be unequally yoked with unbelievers. For what partnership has righteousness with lawlessness? Or what fellowship has light with darkness?" (2 Corinthians 6:14). Now, right up front I'm going to tell you this verse isn't talking about marriage, but the mixing of the Christian faith with other religions. However, that's a very real concern for you when considering serious relationships.

First, when you marry another Christian, it's a comfort for both of you have the same approach to service and station. The world, on the other hand, often pictures marriage as a temporary arrangement you can abandon as soon as things go bad. You do not want to be married to someone who believes it's okay to bug out as soon as they don't feel like being married anymore.

Second, the devil, the world, and your own sinful flesh are all working together to pull you away from Christ. You don't want your spouse to be helping them. I'm not saying you're looking at marrying someone with horns and a pitchfork, but a non-Christian isn't going to understand why you're going to get up early every week and ruin a perfectly good lazy Sunday morning by going off to church. Quiet moments together are tough to find, and they'll be hoping you'll stay home to spend time with them—not because they want to destroy your soul, but because they like you and want to spend time with you. This can lead to two big problems: either you keep going to church and it becomes a sore spot with your spouse, or you stop going to church and shipwreck your faith. It's a whole lot better if the two of you are committed to helping each other hear the Gospel every week. Think it gets better as you grow old and wise? Imagine this situation: an old man who has never been a Christian knows death is near and asks to speak to a pastor. He hears the good news Jesus died for his sins. However, his unbelieving wife has Alzheimer's and is locked in a ward at the nursing home, her brain no longer comprehending. He wants to believe in Jesus and be saved; but if he does, he's also confessing his wife is not saved. This heartbreak is too much for him to bear, so he refuses God's grace. It happens.

Third, you're hopefully going to love your mate very, very much. You do not want to go through life with the knowledge they are going to hell unless they become believers at a future date. In this world, every married couple has to live with the certainty that they'll eventually be separated by death. Unless Jesus returns first, it's unavoidable. It's far worse to live life knowing your spouse would be separated from Christ for eternity.

I plead with you, marry a fellow believer. Marriage is a lifetime commitment. You don't want to be tugged between your spouse and your Lord.

Since the purpose of dating is to find the right one to marry, then yes, you should only date other Christians.

Oh, come on. it's just a fun first date to prom. i should still only date other Christians?

I understand where you're coming from, so let me add three more things:

First, just about every marriage in this nation today started with a first date. The couple usually didn't know they'd eventually be husband and wife. How do you know you're not going to marry your prom date? You don't. This could be the one.

Second, if you don't take this seriously now, when are you going to start? Let's say you're sixteen, statistically speaking, you'll probably be married within nine years. Somewhere along the way, you'll decide you'll start dating only Christians. When? When college starts? Makes sense, but if you haven't already gotten into the habit, you're going to have a tough time starting in college. So when— after college? That makes you about twenty-two or twenty-three years old. According to the averages, you'll be married in 2—3 years. That's not much time to learn to date Christians exclusively, unless you've been doing it all along.

Third, it's just a fun date to prom, but prom dates don't always turn out so fun. Imagine, you—the Christian—go out on the date expecting a dance and a ride home. Your date, who is not a Christian, doesn't have the same moral expectations. For a lot of high schoolers, the night starts with *prom* and ends with *iscuity*, if you know what I mean. You don't want to be in a situation where your date demands sexual privileges because it's what the world expects. Go on dates with people who have the same values and standards. Go on dates with people who have the same faith.

What about missionary dating?

"Missionary dating" is the idea you, a Christian, **209** can date a non-Christian to establish a serious relationship and convert them to Christianity. Sometimes, it works. A lot of times, it doesn't. If you're going to insist on dating a non-Christian, then I would encourage you to decide not to marry unless he becomes a Christian. If you're highly attracted to someone who does not believe, then attend a solid confirmation class together—and be ready to take a broken heart and walk away if the other doesn't embrace the faith. If you don't walk away, be prepared for all those extra challenges you've invited into your future—and understand up front your feelings of love for each other won't make them go away.

i'm a Lutheran.
Should i only date Lutherans?

Ideally, yes. Stop groaning at my narrow-mindedness. Here's why.

It all goes back to the idea your station in dating is "potential spouse," that dating leads to marriage. As a married couple, you want to do things together—and supporting each other in church attendance is important. It's a bummer if you both get up on Sunday morning and then take off to different congregations. You can convert to their denomination, but I wouldn't leave the certainty of the Lord's Word and Sacraments, as taught in Lutheran churches, behind. You can try to convert them, but this might become a big, annoying sore spot.

210

The other thing is, for some reason, married people tend to have babies. Babies need to be baptized—but not all Christian denominations agree. As a pastor, I've seen more than one mom and dad have knock-down drag-out fights over whether or not to baptize the kid, since the Lutheran wants to and the non-Lutheran doesn't. It's ugly to watch. It's even worse when they decide to deprive their child of the certain forgiveness Baptism gives until they can get their disagreements worked out.

When things start to get serious, work this stuff out before you get married. Young couples, loopy in love with each other, always think these religious concerns will just take care of themselves—love will conquer all. They don't and it doesn't. Take care of it now, and you'll thank me later.

Why can't i find anybody nice to date?

I heard one girl ask her friend this very question while I was working at my university office. It's a cool place that looks just like a Starbucks, probably because it is. But anyway, there I was typing away on a sermon and drinking a cup of decaf Verona when this girl at the next table exclaims, "I can't understand it! I keep on going to these drinking parties to meet guys, but every guy I meet just seems to want one thing! (The "one thing," by the way, was not to encourage the girl to lead a chaste and decent life in word and deed, just in case you didn't catch on.) Why can't I meet any nice guys?!" She seemed genuinely perplexed. Imagine, a girl not finding a nice guy at a college drinking party. Shocking!

To put it another way—duh! If you want to find nice people to date, then look for them in nice places. For instance, if your standards include dating a churchgoer then, I don't know, try finding them at church. Duh!

Just to be clear, don't go to church to find dates. Go there for forgiveness. But you might find a fellow penitent there who has the same goals and standards.

Now, even if you're looking in the right places, you may not find the right one right away. Be patient. The Lord knows the plans He has for you (Jeremiah 29:11).

i live in a place where the dating pool isn't very big. it's always just been me

and "Weird Jimmy" in Sunday School, and i still don't find Jimmy's belching his memory work all that attractive. is there hope?

Sure. It's the Lord who gave the gift of marriage, and it's the Lord who made you His own in Holy Baptism. He is working all things for your good (Romans 8:28). As you get older, you'll find more and more people panicking because they haven't found the right person. Surveys and statistics show time is running out. But you're not at the mercy of statistics; you're in the hands of the Lord. I'd suggest keeping busy with other things. Furthermore, pray. Commend your cares to the Lord, confess your worry and impatience, and pray for your future spouse, whoever that person may be. The Lord delights to hear your prayers, and He will answer as is best for you (1 Peter 5:6–7).

i know this girl, and we've been friends for a while. i've thought about asking her out, but she's not that pretty. Any advice?

I suppose you're just ruggedly handsome with 7% body fat? Listen, the world puts a huge emphasis on looks and beauty. Yet again, I point you back to Proverbs 31:30, "Charm is deceitful, and beauty is vain, but a woman who fears the Lord is to be praised." Beauty comes and goes; a faithful woman is to be treasured.

Having said this, I think there's nothing wrong with you and her—and me, for that matter—trying to look as good as we can. Proper hygiene, for instance, can do a lot. So can diet and exercise. Sometimes it can't. Sometimes, it's a medical problem or we just don't have the looks we wish we had.

But when it comes to personal improvement, your personal appearance is your responsibility. Her personal appearance is hers. If you can't get over the fact she's not as pretty as you'd like, then don't ask her out. Bear in mind, however, she's not the one who's being shallow. This is your hang-up, not hers. On the other hand, if someone says, "Now that I've got me a mate, I don't have to keep myself up anymore," that's selfish thinking on their part.

213

We've been dating for a while, and i just don't feel the same way i used to. i feel like breaking up. What do i do?

First off, you should figure out why you feel this way. This is about emotions, so think it through.

One thought is emotions take energy. Have you been sick or run-down or busier than usual? If you're low on physical energy, you're going to be low on emotional energy, too. Have you suffered some sort of loss that might cause you to grieve or be depressed? Depression isn't selective. You're either depressed about everything or you're not. It may be you don't feel a lot about the other person because you just don't feel a lot about anything right now.

Or it could be your relationship has been mostly about how you feel about each other. Now you've been going out for a while, the emotion is starting to wear off and there's not a whole lot else that's holding you together.

What do you do? Remember, serving strengthens a relationship. If you want the relationship to continue, then you need to work harder at taking care of the other. If you don't want to put that work into it, then the relationship is going to die.

Remember how you feel right now, though, when you get serious enough to think about getting married. Make sure it's more than feelings that have you considering marriage because sooner or later after the wedding (usually about two years), the feelings are going to fade. If you're working hard to serve each other, you'll be okay. If you're not, you're in for an unpleasant time.

214

My girlfriend wants to break things off, but i want to keep trying. How can i make this work?

Unfortunately, you can't. For a relationship to work, both have to be working hard. If one of you doesn't want to be in the relationship, then it's not a relationship anymore. If she's only thinking about breaking up, you can talk and see how to repair things. But if she's made up her mind, I don't see much hope.

We've been dating for a while, and i think we're getting serious— maybe even talking engagement. What does this mean?

It means you've pretty much stepped past the scope of this book, but that won't stop me from yapping a little bit, anyway. It means, along with everything else, you'll want to be sure to look into the future as far as you can to make sure that you have common goals. Do you both want to have kids? How many? If you have kids, will mom stay home or keep working? If you're both working and one of you gets transferred to a different state, whose job comes first? Where do you plan to live? How much time will you spend with relatives? What do you see as the greatest challenges and threats to a happy marriage? The questions go on and on.

Find a good pastor and talk to him. Having said this, I'll add this disclaimer; as a pastor, I'm not a licensed counselor or psychologist. If there are significant challenges (one of you comes from an abusive situation or there are a lot of divorces in the family), it may be very wise for you to spend the money and time to work through some of these things before you get married and these issues become problems between the two of you. Don't just pick one out of the phone book, though. Your pastor might have a good name in mind.

216 One Final Answer One More Time

Still have questions? Me too! You always will. That's because relationships involve people, and people are always changing. Relationships change—sometimes for the better, sometimes for the worse. The questions will keep coming, and remember: for every one of those infinite questions, there are even more answers. It's just that most of the answers are wrong.

So over the past nine chapters, I've tried to do more than just answer a bunch of random questions. I've also tried to lay down some basic truths that don't change. Keep these in mind, and you're prepared to answer the questions that come your way. Here are a few we've covered:

* God is the ultimate authority, and He has the final say.

* God tells you His final say in His Word.

* Honor authorities, unless they command you to disobey God.

* In every relationship, you're to be a servant.

217

* By nature, you're selfish. Confess it and be forgiven.

* By nature, everybody else is selfish, too.

* Life isn't fair. Don't expect it to be.

* You're going to have enemies.

* Don't follow your feelings,
  since they'll be different
  tomorrow.

* Trust has to be earned.

Keep these in mind and use them as an anchor because they're not going to change.

But more than all of these, remember this—remember God's relationship to you. "He who did not spare His own Son but gave Him up for us all, how will He not also with Him graciously give us all things?" (Romans 8:32) There will be times when you're on top of the world and times you'll be hoping for the earth to swallow you—usually because of relationships. But this doesn't change:

> ✱ God the Father gave up His own Son for you.
>
> ✱ The Son went willingly to the cross to redeem you.
>
> ✱ The Holy Spirit made you a child of God by Baptism, and continues to serve you by visiting you with grace and life.

No matter what else happens, the Lord says to you, "Fear not, for I have redeemed you; I have called you by name, you are mine" (Isaiah 43:1).

Now, *that's* a comforting relationship. And it's *never* going to change.

Notes

Notes

Notes